Computing & Information TECHNOLOGY

DANTES/DSST* Test Study Guide

> All rights reserved. This Study Guide, Book and Flashcards are protected under the US Copyright Law. No part of this book or study guide or flashcards may be reproduced, distributed or stored in a retrieval system, or transmitted in any form or by any means, electronic, mechanical, photocopying, recording, or otherwise, without the prior written permission of the publisher Breely Crush Publishing, LLC.

© 2026 Breely Crush Publishing, LLC

*DSST is a registered trademark of The Thomson Corporation and its affiliated companies, and does not endorse this book.

971050324143

Copyright ©2003 - 2026, Breely Crush Publishing, LLC.

All rights reserved.

This Study Guide, Book and Flashcards are protected under the US Copyright Law. No part of this publication may be reproduced, distributed or stored in a retrieval system, or transmitted in any form or by any means, electronic, mechanical, photocopying, recording, or otherwise, without the prior written permission of the publisher Breely Crush Publishing, LLC.

Published by Breely Crush Publishing, LLC
10808 River Front Parkway
South Jordan, UT 84095
www.breelycrushpublishing.com

ISBN-13: 978-1-61433-660-0

Printed and bound in the United States of America.

**DSST is a registered trademark of The Thomson Corporation and its affiliated companies, and does not endorse this book.*

Table of Contents

Computer Hardware and Functions 1
    Computer Contifurations 2
    Computer Devices 2
Digital Representation 5
Personal Communications 6
Network and Client/Server Architectures 7
Networks 8
Relevance to Business 10
    Local Area Network and Nodes 14
    Network Cabling 17
    Communications Protocol 18
    Modem and Fax 18
Operating Systems 19
Software Development Methods & Tools 21
    Methods 21
    Tools 23
    Pseudocode 23
    Conversion to a New System 26
Programming Languages 27
    Categories of High Level Languages 28
    CGI Interface 29
User Interfaces 30
Software Packages 31
Software Development 32
Data Management 33
    Hypertext and Hypermedia 33
    Database Management Systems 34
    Data Concepts and Data Structures 35
    Document Images 36
    Units of Measurement 37
    File Names 37
Information Processing Management 37
    System Development Processes 37
    Types of Information Processing Applications 38
    Standards 38
Security and Controls 39
Information Processing Careers 40

Applications in Organizations	*41*
Management Decision Making	*41*
User Applications	*42*
Office Systems	*42*
Internet and the World Wide Web	*43*
Zombie and Slave Computers	*47*
Email	*48*
History of Computing	*48*
Significant People in Computing	*51*
Social and Ethical Issues	*52*
Business Ethics	*54*
Software Licensing	*58*
Safety and Security for Networks	*58*
Mobile Networks	*59*
Programming Methodology	*59*
Data Types and Algorithms	*60*
Program Concepts	*62*
Logic Concepts	*64*
Software Development Tools	*65*
Sample Test Questions	*67*
Test Taking Strategies	*97*
Test Preparation	*97*
Legal Note	*98*

 Computer Hardware and Functions

The term computer hardware refers to any of the electronic components that make up the computer, such as the monitor, the CPU, the disk drives, or the printer. Hardware is separate from software, the general term for any program that performs calculations and controls what you see on the monitor. A computer comes with some basic software when it is purchased; this software is known as the operating system. An operating system (OS) is a master control program that oversees all computer functions and manages how information is placed onto the various hardware devices. Microsoft Windows is an example of a popular operating system.

The computer's CPU, also known as the central processing unit, is the primary microprocessor that governs the computer's operations. Most personal computers (PC's) rely on microprocessors manufactured by Intel, such as the Pentium or Celeron processor. The CPU's speed directly impacts the performance of software programs. The CPU comprises three essential components: an arithmetic logic unit, a control unit, and a set of registers.

The CPU, or Central Processing Unit, is famed for being the "brain" of the computer. It is a small piece on the inside of the computer which is essentially responsible for running the whole computer. It processes the information and instructions given to it by programs to allow computer users to do anything from writing papers to playing games. Everything that the computer does goes through the CPU, making it a very important element. The CPU has four main functions. They are fetch, decode, execute, and writeback.

Fetch describes the CPU's search for the information it needs. Sometimes, it searches through the RAM, program memory, or hard drive. As the CPU goes through a step-by-step process, it must fetch the information it needs for each step.

Once the CPU has fetched the information, it must decode it. The language computerwork in is binary code, a series of 0s and 1s. Different languages have been developed because writing programs in binary code would take so much time and effort. The computer has to translate programs into binary code because they are written in these different languages. This is done through the use of compilers.

Based on the instructions which have been decoded, the CPU can then execute the instructions. For example, a person types 24/6 into their computer's built-in calculator function. This command goes to the CPU (the fetch stage). It is then translated into binary code which the CPU understands (the decode stage). It recognizes that division is needed to solve the problem and uses preprogrammed division logic to come up with the answer: four.

Having the answer, it moves to the last step, writeback. In the writeback stage the CPU produces output. In this case, the output is displaying the number four, but depending on the command it was given, the output could be any number of things. Once the CPU has finished the cycle, it starts again with another task or step.

Pipelining refers to a CPU's ability to process more than one task at a time. The pipeline will divide into segments, with each designated a different task. One will fetch and pass it on to the next, and fetch again, while their other segments work on it. This way the CPU works faster and more efficiently.

Every computer has an **instruction set**, which is a list of keywords that corresponds to all of the operations that the CPU contains. CPU's can be a **complex instruction set computer (CISC)** that support approximately 100 instructions for greater speed or a **reduced instruction set computer (RISC)** with a minimal set of instructions designed for a specialized application. **Registers** are specialized storage areas that store values while the instructions operate upon them. The **arithmetic logic unit (ALU)** is the component of the CPU that supports the standard arithmetic functions like add and subtract as well as logical operations like AND and OR. The **control unit** is the electronic controller over the operations that the instructions perform much like the brain controls our actions.

COMPUTER CONFIGURATIONS

A personal computer (PC) is a small computer equipped with its own operating system and peripheral devices typically needed by one individual. PCs are differentiated from a personal digital assistant (PDA), which is a hand-held computer customized for everyday functions for personal organization, such as an appointment calendar, an address book, a notepad, and fax or other two-way messaging capability.

Large companies historically have relied upon some form of mainframe computer to handle their voluminous data processing needs. A mainframe computer is a multi-user computer capable of simultaneously processing thousands of calculations. Mainframe computers were the primary type of computers available from the 1960s onward.

COMPUTER DEVICES

Another critical hardware device is the hard disk or disk drive. The hard disk is an electronic component of the computer that is used for storing information. It may also be called a hard drive. The hard disk offers RAM, which means data can be read from and written to this device. RAM is distinguished from ROM memory found in the

CPU; ROM memory is read-only. It makes sense that parts of the operating system are read-only; that is, nothing else can be written over the basics of the operating system. The computer will no longer operate properly if the operating system is destroyed. Volatile memory is any type of memory that is erased when the computer is turned off. For example, RAM empties when the computer is turned off. This is why files must be saved on a hard drive or to another permanent memory device. However, this doesn't make the RAM useless – it is very helpful in speeding up computer functions.

A cache is a small memory unit used by the CPU. Level 1 cache, or L1 cache, is generally built into the CPU, and the level 2, or L2 cache, is generally attached to the motherboard. The caches store information about programs. When the request for the information comes up, the CPU can find it much faster than if it had to search the RAM or hard drive. The CPU first searches the L1 cache, then the L2 cache, and if it isn't in either place, it will proceed to the RAM. Multiple small caches are used instead of one large cache because the smaller they are, the faster the CPU can search them.

The hard disk is an integral part of the computer and is portable only to the extent that the computer itself is portable, such as a notebook or laptop PC.

Alternate drives are available to handle portable information storage devices such as floppy disks, diskettes, or CDs. Floppy disks are 5.25-inch portable storage devices that are mostly out-of-date today, while diskettes are 3.5 inches wide and encased in plastic. Neither of these is typically used anymore.

CDs or compact disks replaced disks as the latest in portable information devices. These were soon replaced by DVDs, which can hold much more data. Blu-ray is a new type of disc with a higher storage capacity than CDs or DVDs, which makes it useful for high-definition videos. Part of the reason it is able to do this is because while regular DVDs are read using a red laser, Blu-ray discs are read with a blue laser. Blue lasers have a shorter wavelength than red lasers and can read more closely packed information.

All storage devices can be divided into files, which represent individual documents or other collections of information identified by unique names.

The computer user communicates with the software and CPU by entering information through a keyboard, which is called an input device because it is used to enter information into the computer. The keyboard provides alphabetic, numeric, punctuation, symbols, and control keys. When a key is depressed, an electronic signal that is unique to the key is sent to the CPU. The operating system typically displays the associated letter, number, or symbol on the monitor, a piece of hardware resembling a television screen. Monitors use screen resolution, also called display resolution, to describe the clarity of a screen. Screen resolution is defined in terms of pixels. A pixel is a specific point on the screen. Therefore, the more pixels, the higher the quality of the images will be.

The refresh rate, or vertical refresh rate, describes the number of times per second that a computer screen is redrawn or updated. It is measured in hertz (Hz). Typically, a refresh rate lower than 60 Hz will have a noticeable flicker. However, as refresh rates increase, this does not always produce a noticeable difference.

The computer user also enters information by using a communication device known as a mouse. A mouse is another input device. This device fits easily in the human hand and is designed to roll on a flat surface that roughly translates to the monitor's area. The mouse is used to locate an area the user is interested in on the monitor. Clicking the buttons on the mouse is a typical method for selecting options that are displayed on the monitor by software programs.

The keyboard, monitor and mouse are the primary peripheral devices that are used for entering information into the computer. A **peripheral device** is any electronic component that is attached to the computer but external to it. Another external peripheral device is a **scanner**, which is used to copy paper documents or pictures into memory on the hard drive. A touch screen is another input device that is used in applications that are available to a general user. The **touch screen** enters the user's choices based upon a simple pressing of the indicated area of the pressure-sensitive panel. **Bar code readers** are used in business applications to interpret bar codes that indicate what the product is, and they are particularly important in warehousing applications. A **point-of-sale (POS) terminal** is a computerized cash register that allows the input of data such as item sold, price, and method of payment. **Digital cameras** can now be connected directly to a personal computer for downloading pictures onto the hard disk. Most also have the option of removing additional storage via a memory card which can be inserted into a card reader to access the information. Most PCs now come equipped with media card readers included. A scanner is an input device. It is used to get an image from paper to the computer screen.

Just as there are a variety of peripheral devices for input, there are also numerous **output devices,** that is, components whose main purpose is to retrieve processed information that is stored in the computer's memory. The most familiar output device is a **printer**, which produces a paper copy of the desired document, picture, or graphs. Some printers are now special purpose devices that are designed only to print pictures. The computer **monitor** serves as an output device when it is used to retrieve information that is stored in memory. The **PC speakers** are also an output device for audio messages that accompany software systems or that are recorded on Internet web sites.

Printers, fax machines and scanners are different input and output devices used in transferring data to and from computers. A printer is an output machine. It is linked to the computer and reproduces images on paper in either color or black and white. A fax machine processes input, such as text, and sends it over a phone line to another computer.

Digital Representation

Computers are electronic and can only store information as a group of binary digits that is composed of 0's and 1's only. Each binary digit is known as a bit. Eight consecutive bits in computer memory are called a byte.

Our normal arithmetic is base 10 or decimal, with digits 0-9 only. Binary arithmetic within the computer is base 2, with digits 0-1 only. So decimal 0 is 0 binary, 1 is 1, but 2 is 10 binary, and 3 is 11 binary, 4 is 100 binary and so on. While the internal computer performs numeric calculations in binary, the operating system converts the internal binary to the decimal system we are accustomed to whenever the numbers are sent to an output device such as the monitor or printer. Sometimes, very large numbers are stored in the computer in a form known as binary-coded decimal (BCD), where each decimal digit is stored as a 4-bit binary number.

How are letters or text stored? The letters that come in as electronic signals from the keyboard are converted to Extended Binary Coded Decimal Interchange Code (EBCDIC) for IBM mainframe computers and American Standard Code for Information Interchange (ASCII) for personal computers. The basic idea for these codes is that every letter of the alphabet and every other symbol, like the punctuation marks and percent sign, are converted to a binary code that fits into an 8-bit byte; however, ASCII coding uses only 7 of the 8 bits. These byte-oriented encoding schemes can handle 256 possible characters and symbols and thus are not suited for languages that have more symbols, like some of the Oriental languages.

Pictures have their own graphics digital representation or Joint Photographic Experts Group (JPEG) format. This format can represent up to 16.7 million color variations for each pixel or picture element. JPEG images are best used in the case of photographs or other images which require smooth color transitions and patterns. They are often used as the files created when you take a picture with a digital camera. JPEGs are also useful for Internet purposes because they can compress well.

GIF images are used for images with sharp contrast between colors, such as with animations or logos. They can also be used as short, low resolution video clips.

PNG files were actually designed to replace GIFs. They do not, however, support animations. They do have a larger color range than GIFs do, and they are better with gradual color changes.

A pixel is the smallest picture element that an output device can handle. A pixel is the smallest identifiable element on a computer screen. Essentially, what is seen on a computer screen is the result of millions of pixels being manipulated to create a display. The resolution, or clarity, of the screen is determined by the amount of pixels there are. The more pixels there are, the higher the resolution is. The higher the resolution is, the sharper the image. For example, a computer with resolution 1360 x 900 would have over 1.2 million pixels, 1,224,000 pixels to be exact. However, a computer with 640 x 480 resolution would have only 307,000 total pixels.

A picture is composed of a grid of pixels. Another picture format is **Tagged Image File Format (TIFF)** that is used for scanned photographic images. Graphs and graphics files are compressed using **Graphics Interchange Format (GIF)**. Video has its own format as well, namely the **Moving Picture Experts Group (MPEG)** format which provides for the compression of digitized videos and animation. **Vector Graphics** are images generated from mathematical descriptions of where line length, positioning and other shapes should be. Raster graphics programs produce **bitmaps (BMP)** which are details of each row and column of pixel.

MPEG files are higher quality digital videos.

MP3 files are audio files.

Audio files are often put into this file format to be transferred from one computer (or device) to another.

BIF files are Boot Information Files. They are used to boot a computer from a disc. DOC files, or documents, are word processing files.

 Personal Communications

Email or electronic mail is text sent between two computers. There are many free and paid email sources; the largest free email service providers are Hotmail, Google Mail (or Gmail), and Yahoo. Email is one of the quickest, least expensive, and easiest ways to stay in touch. When emailing an attachment (a photo, document, or anything other than text) to someone, the file may be too large for you to send. To make the file size smaller, you may need to compress it using a program like WinZip. By zipping a file, you are compressing it, i.e., making it smaller. The "zipped" file would have the extension .zip. When the recipient receives the email attachment, they must use a "zipping" or archive program to unpack or unzip the file.

Chat groups are another way to communicate with people. In a chat group, people post messages on a forum or bulletin board online. Then, they respond to other posted messages that they are interested in. This is much slower than instant messaging, which is a newer, more real-time way to communicate online. Whatever you type is posted immediately to a window on the computer containing who you are communicating with. This can be a private conversation or involve several other people.

There are many types of chat forums, and they all have different levels of privacy and content. A blog is basically an online journal or webpage where a person (or company) posts anything from a quick note to their favorite new links. This is akin to a daily column in a newspaper. Blogs can be updated as much as the owner wants, monthly, daily, or bi-weekly. Blogging has encouraged many would-be writers to post their own thoughts and essays online. A newsgroup is where a group of people get together to discuss a topic such as auto racing or dieting. These groups are usually unmoderated (meaning no one screens what is posted) and are usually free for people to join and contribute to. A newsgroup can use a list server, which is a way for one person to create a single email, which is then sent to the entire group.

Network and Client/Server Architectures

The term telecommunications originated in the transmission of computer data over the public telephone network. Today, the term refers to the broader scope of transmitting computer data over any network. What is a network? A network is a broader computer system created when ,cables link two or more computers together and each computer needs to be equipped with a network interface card to plug in the cables. The computers can also be connected to a wireless network, where each computer has a wireless network adapter that is equipped with an antenna.

All the computers that are connected to the same network are said to be on the network and can be called a network node. When a node is active on the network,, it is onlin; whenen it is n, it it is offline. A computer can be offline due to the request of the user or due to some type of computer or network malfunction. Networking is a way to share files of information, share resources like printers, use one master copy of a software program, or send messages. Once a computer is a network node, it is technically no longer a "personal" computer because some resources are shared with others.

Networks

A computer network may involve as few as three computers. The Internet is a network of millions of computers and servers. Each computer within a network is called a node.

Networks come in many configurations:

- **Mesh:** Every computer in the network is linked to every other computer.
- **Star:** There is a central computer. Every other computer in the network is linked to the central computer.
- **Hierarchy:** One node is linked to several child nodes. Each of these is the parent to another level of nodes.
- **Bus:** Each computer is linked linearly to a single communication channel ("bus").
- **Ring:** Computers are linked circularly to a single communication channel.
- **Hybrid:** Networks are linked in a combination of two or more structures.

Structure	*Advantage*	*Disadvantage*
Mesh	Quick and efficient data transmission	Adding new nodes difficult
Star	Data travels only a short distance	Entire network down if central computer fails
Hierarchy	More reliable, as network can survive if a lower level node fails	Data must travel longer distance, therefore slower data flow

Bus	Reliable, network very resilient if any computer fails	Very slow data flow
Ring	Reliable, as in a bus configuration	Slow

Network designs work on a continuum of reliability and speed. The most reliable configurations are usually the slowest. Hybrid systems try to maximize the benefits of two or more designs.

Wide Area Networks and Internetworks

WANs may be star, hierarchical or hybrid configurations and may include many types of computers. Internetworks are used to connect individual LANs and WANs. Connections between similar networks, such as two LANs, are achieved through a **bridge**. Two different networks, a LAN and a WAN for instance, are linked with a **gateway**. A **router** is used to direct messages to the correct destinations throughout the connected networks.

The **Internet** is a public internetwork which contains a collection of web pages, each identified by a unique uniform resource locator (URL). The Internet has become so popular, that many organizations use an **intranet**, which is a network based on the Internet but limited to internal users.

In addition to classifications of networks, there are also many elements within a network that require explanation. Although some networks connect through token ring topology, in which devices are connected in a circle, many topologies connect through hubs. The computers and other devices are all connected directly to the hub, and thereby indirectly connected to each other. Switches perform a similar function as hubs in that they can be used to connect computers in a network. However, they can generate increased productivity because they allow for two way communication, meaning that messages can be sent and received at the same time. Another advantage over hubs is that switches allow data to be transferred directly between two computers, rather than broadcasted over an entire network.

Routers and firewalls are used to regulate the connections between networks. Routers establish a connection between networks and then regulate the traffic over that connection. One common use of a router is to connect a school or office network to the Internet (which is a network itself). The router transmits data between the two, and can deny access where necessary. A firewall is a device which prevents unauthorized access to a network. Because routers can deny access to a network they function as one type of firewall, but the classification includes many additional functions. Firewalls are specifically created to protect a network and screen all of the data, either sent or received, that passes through it.

Relevance to Business

Networks may be divided into two general types based on their size. A **local area network (LAN)** covers a small geographic area, for example a hospital campus or an office building. **Wide area networks (WANs)** cover large geographic areas, for example a city or several countries. **Internetworks** are comprised of connected LANs and WANs.

Local Area Networks

LANs can be wired or wireless. They are usually ring or bus networks and require specialized hardware and software. A network interface card (NIC) connects a computer to the communications channel. Applications are needed to allow the node to send and receive information across the network.

A LAN may include resource servers that can be accessed by the client computers:

- **Print server:** Allows every computer connected to the server to share the printer.
- **File server:** Allows connected computers to share a secondary storage device.
- **Database server:** Server connected to a secondary storage device used in database processing throughout the LAN.

LANs can be an effective and efficient way for users throughout an organization to share information and resources. Client/server systems, where data is stored in a centralized database on the server then sent to client computers as users require it, are often preferred over multiple-user computer systems for many reasons:

- In client/server environments, the server does not handle the data processing, database management or user interface. This allows the organization to buy a smaller computer to act as a server than would be required for the central computer of a comparable multiple-user system.
- It is cheaper and easier to add new client computers as the company grows than it is to add additional multiple-user computers.

WANs

WANs are often preferred by businesses that have operations separated by long distances. WANS may be based on public or private communication networks. Depending on the size of the area that needs to be connected, businesses may purchase their own cables or wireless system, or they can lease long-distance channels – usually the more economical choice for networks that span very large areas.

Businesses may choose to purchase the hardware and software required to connect to a WAN, or they may contract long-distance links and value-added networks with a communications company. A value-added network (VAN) includes additional software and hardware the company may find useful.

Businesses may choose to use the Internet instead of a common carrier channel or VAN. In this case, security measures such as data encryption and user authentication may be needed to protect company information and correspondence.

Electronic Commerce

Organizations often use networks to facilitate electronic commerce (e-commerce). E-commerce involves a **web server**, which stores the pages of the business's website and is equipped with specialized software. An organization may use its own web server or one provided by an Internet service provider (ISP).

A web server is often linked to a database server by a LAN. The database server contains information necessary for e-commerce; for example, product availability and prices. A customer initiates an e-commerce transaction by accessing the business's website. When a customer places an order, the web server uses information from the database server to process orders. The order information is sent back to the customer.

Security

Organizations need to keep their information secure while it is being stored ("at rest"), and when it is being transferred across a network ("in motion"). Federal, state, local and industrial regulations set standards for adequate security. Organizations that are not compliant with these ordinances may face legal sanctions and fines.

Records that should be protected includes information about customers, employees and business processes. In addition, organizations often want to protect their financial records, business processes, marketing strategies and future plans.

Information security breaches can be the result of either malicious or nonmalicious attacks. Malicious attacks, those that are intended to gain access to or harm secure information, may be the work of hacking, disgruntled employees, organized crime or espionage. Nonmalicious attacks are often caused by careless employees and poorly trained system users.

There are five classes of attacks identified by the National Security Agency:
- **Passive attacks** include capturing passwords or other data by monitoring communications.
- **Active attacks** cause corrupted files, denial of service or information disclosure by overriding security systems or introducing malicious programs.
- **Close-in attacks** require the physical presence of the attacker to access information or to corrupt files.
- **Insider attacks** are those by people within the organization.
- **Distribution attacks** are malicious changes in the system hardware or software during distribution or construction. For example, a programmer may leave a "back door" in an application to allow future access to the system.

Organizations attempt to protect themselves from attacks by using physical, administrative and technological safeguards.

Physical Security

Most security breaches can be prevented by adequate physical safeguards. Physical security attempts to prevent the theft and loss of hardware and storage media. Some physical security measures include:
- Limited offsite transport of equipment and disks
- Secure disposal of retired equipment
- Monitored use of equipment

Administrative Security

Administrative safeguards include written policies and procedures addressing issues such as:
- What to do if a data breach is suspected
- Security training
- Who may have access to what data

- Current and future protection needs
- Sanctions if security policies are broken by employees

Technological Security

Technological security includes hardware and software used to keep in motion and at rest data safe. These measures may include:

- Password systems
- Two-way handshakes
- Three-way handshakes
- Digital signatures
- Centralized logging
- External authentication

Password Systems

Password systems require users to log in before using selected applications or accessing data. An intercepted password, or a password that has been discovered through a brute force method, make the system vulnerable to access by unauthorized users. In a **brute force attack**, malicious attackers attempt to discover a password by trying all possible combinations.

Organizations can make password systems more effective by:

- Requiring each user to have a unique username and related password. This also allows for better tracking of who is accessing what information.
- Requiring passwords to be longer than a certain number of characters and to contain numbers, letter and symbols. This increases the number of possible passwords, therefore decreasing the likelihood of a brute force attack finding a password.
- Automatically logging users out when the session becomes inactive.
- Randomly assigning passwords or requiring periodic password changes. Users may be relying on the same password for multiple systems. If one password is intercepted, multiple systems may be vulnerable.
- Using encryption whenever passwords are transmitted across the network.

Handshakes

Handshakes are the exchange of information between different elements of a system in order to confirm authorization before accessing and transmitting information.

In a two-way handshake, the equipment or application requesting data sends an electronic code. Another code is sent by the system element from which data is being requested. Before any information is transmitted, both codes are verified. A three-way handshake requires another verified code from the requestor before data can be transmitted.

Digital Signatures

Digital signatures authenticate data transfers through the use of mathematical algorithms. The transmitting element in the system signs the data transfer using a secret formula, the "private key." The receiving element verifies that the signature is authentic using an open "public" key. Digital signatures can be used to verify that changes to data files are from authorized users. This can help maintain the integrity of an information system.

Centralized Logging

Centralized logging involves the recording of every entry to, access of, and change within a system. Periodical auditing of the logs can reveal unauthorized users and security flaws. Monitoring logs can help detect brute force attacks before they are successful.

External Authentication

External authentication relies on a remote service to determine if users should have access to a system. External systems can offer flexibility for the system manager and convenience for the users. Users only have to log in once to access any information they need, and are authorized for, on the server.

LOCAL AREA NETWORK AND NODES

A **local area network (LAN)** is a network of nodes that are in close physical proximity. Network nodes are generally tied together with network cables; however, with advances in technology, many LAN's are migrating towards wireless technology. In a wired network, a hardware device known as a **network hub** is needed as a central location for the wiring and all network nodes are connected to this central hub.

There are two main **LAN architectures**: peer-to-peer and client/server. In **peer-to-peer** architecture, all the nodes have access to the public files on every other node; in effect, all nodes are equal peers. In **client/server** architecture, one central computer is called the server. The server holds the central files and software and the client programs residing on the computers in the network access and modify the data that is on the server. This is the network architecture that is used by most business applications today. The main database is stored on the **server** computer and numerous workers access this data from network nodes. Picture an insurance company that has a customer service call center. Any customer service representative can answer a call and retrieve a policy holder's status from the server and update the information as required.

In a particular network, there can be more than one computer that is designated as a server. It is best that each server is dedicated to a particular function. A **file server** is a computer on the client/server network that stores the application programs and data files that are used by the workstations in the network. In a peer-to-peer network, every workstation functions as a file server because all other network nodes can access the public files on every other network node. A file server is responsible for **locking** data to keep multiple network nodes from attempting to update the same data simultaneously. A **mainframe** is a very large computer that can support thousands of users at a time.

A **print server** is a computer that is dedicated solely to managing the flow of output files to one or more printers. A print server is needed by companies that use expensive printers because they generate lots of documents and reports. While the same computer can be used as both a file server and a print server, it is usually recommended that these two functions be placed on separate computers when there are numerous network nodes.

For specialized large business applications, a file server might be coupled with a database server. While a file server holds all kinds of files and may contain database files, a **database server** contains only the major database files for the large application. A dedicated computer is needed to process the large database files efficiently.

Companies with a significant Internet presence will also dedicate a **web server** to their web site. Similarly, another server can be dedicated to e-mail messaging and it is called a **mail server**. The e-mail handling program on the workstations must be compatible with the e-mail handling software on the server.

The terminology for clients and servers becomes fuzzy because it applies to both hardware and database applications. In hardware terms, server can mean any computer that is dedicated as a file server, a print server, a database server, a web server or a mail server or in software terms it can mean any computer that has the main application program and database. However, the term client usually applies only to the software programs that reside on the workstations in the network, which may be called client workstations or client computers. Be sure to read questions on the exam referring to client/server carefully and remember that the server is in charge, controlling all updates to the database it holds. Clients are the workstations or the computers that hold the client software; clients send requests for information or database updates (changes) to the server.

Along with two forms of architecture are three forms of network topology. The term **network topology** refers to the arrangement of nodes as either centralized or decentralized. In a centralized or **star network,** all the nodes are connected to a central computer that controls all access to the network. While this form of LAN provides greater security and central management, a star network is expensive to install because each node requires a separate cable link to the hub. In a decentralized topology, nodes are connected together directly.

In a **bus network,** the nodes are connected one to the next in a continuous fashion. This is very inexpensive but if any connection between two nodes fails, the entire network fails. The final traditional form of network topology is the decentralized **ring network** which is a bus network where the last node is connected to the first node, forming a loop. With the capability of two-way communication, any break in the connection no longer takes down the network.

Since computers in network are no longer functioning as personal computers, a regular operating system like Windows that controls only directly connected peripherals is no longer adequate. Any personal computers that are in network require a network operating system. A **network operating system (NOS)** has features for administering the network (keeping track of users and connections), back-up features for the server, security restrictions, and software for controlling the shared usage of peripheral devices.

The NOS is also responsible for handling all communications between the computers in the network, which also may be called **workstations** in network terminology. Windows NT is an example of a network operating system. Windows Server, Novell Netware and Linux are examples of network operating systems for client/server networks.

After all this discussion, what are the necessary features of a network? The network requires two or more computers that are linked together with a network operating system that provides a **network protocol**, which is the method that the operating system uses to lock data.

There needs to be cabling or wireless connections between the network nodes and the operating system must provide a means of sharing the peripheral devices, which may also be called input and output media. Finally, every node in the network needs to have a unique identifier or **network address** that differentiates it from every other network node. While most networks in operation today use dedicated servers, a server is not required, especially for peer-to-peer networks.

The **network protocol** is a method for controlling a workstation's access to the public data on the network. For example, two users cannot be updating the same file at the same time. Why would two users want the same file? Much of software development is done by a team of programmers and several team members might need to work on the same document, each adding their own chapter, for example. If the network didn't enforce file locking, when it comes time to save the latest copy, one person's updates could be overwritten by someone else.

Carrier sense multiple access with collision detection (CSMA/CD) is one method for controlling access to public data. Using this method, each network node has an equal right to access the communication channel to the public data. If two nodes attempt to access the same data simultaneously, the network operating system decides which request to honor first by generating a random number. This method works quite well for small- to medium-size networks.

However, for large networks, other access methods are used. **Token passing** requires the implementation of a **token**, which is a particular pattern of bits; the token is passed like a baton in a relay race from workstation to workstation. Only the network node that currently has the "baton" or token is allowed to send or receive public data on the network. Like CSMA/CD, token passing gives equal opportunity to send and receive data to all network nodes. **TELNET** is a way to access remote computers.

NETWORK CABLING

Before the advent of today's wireless technology, all networks required cables that physically attached the network nodes, also called workstations or just computers, together for a peer-to-peer network or to a central hub or network server in a client/server architecture. Many existing networks still use cabling, as do many new in-office networks. The cabling is not out-of-date just yet.

Several standards defines network cabling. You simply can't just plug one device into another and expect them to communicate. Remember that the operating system of the computers, both workstations, and servers, must be able to translate the signals to achieve proper communication between all nodes of the network as well as with the peripheral devices.

Historically, there are three standards for network cabling: ARCnet, Ethernet, and token ring. ARCnet is an older version of networking that was developed for the original IBM personal or mainframe computers and supported a star topology, a token-passing protocol, twisted pair or coaxial cable, and ARCnet network interface cards. A token ring network is a combination of a ring and star topology that uses a token-passing network protocol and twisted pair cable. IBM introduced This network form in 1986 and supported 255 workstations.

Today, most businesses use the Ethernet cabling standard, developed by Xerox Corporation. An Ethernet network can have up to 1,024 network nodes in a bus topology. Ethernet uses carrier sense multiple access with collision detection (CSMA/CD).

One of the latest forms of high-speed cabling for sophisticated networks is fiber-optic cable, which is constructed from thin fibers of glass rather than copper wire like twisted-pair cables. Laser light is transmitted, and at the receiving end, optical detectors transform the light into digital signals. Fiber-optic cable is currently both expensive and difficult to work with.

COMMUNICATIONS PROTOCOL

When information is passed between network nodes or transferred from one computer to another via telecommunications, a **communications protocol** or standard is required so that both computers understand the signals and treat them the same way. There are several communication protocols in use today:

- **Asynchronous** – the transmission of bits is not synchronized by a clock signal but is accomplished by sending the bits one after another, with a start and stop bit to mark the beginning and end of each data unit. Telephone lines can be used for this protocol.
- **Synchronous** – data is transmitted at very high speeds by using circuits that synchronize data transfer with electronic clock signals. Computers in high-speed mainframe networks use this protocol.
- **Full-duplex** – asynchronous transmission that allows the communications channel to send and receive signals at the same time.
- **Half-duplex** – also called local echo; asynchronous transmission that can handle only one signal at a time, alternating between the two computers.
- **Double-duplex** – full-duplex transmission with a sender and a receiver at each end that transmits simultaneously in both directions.
- **Echoplex** – the receiving computer acknowledges that it received the data by echoing the data back to the transmitting computer.
- **Parallel** – synchronous transmission through a parallel port to a peripheral device that is usually a parallel printer; the printer signals whether or not it is ready to receive additional data.

MODEM AND FAX

A modem is a peripheral device that sends signals from one computer to another over the telephone lines. The term modem stands for modulator/demodulator. Originally, a modem was an external device, but today's personal computers are sold with built-in modems. The modem has a fixed speed at which it is designed to transmit digital data that converts to analog signals before transmission. Analog signals are sound-based signals that can be transmitted over the telephone lines. At the other end, the signals are again converted from analog to digital.

A fax machine is an electronic device that transmits or receives an image of a printed page over the telephone line. It can also be connected as a shared peripheral device in a network or have fax capability incorporated into a fax modem.

Operating Systems

The **operating system** is the base software of the computer that deals directly with the basic hardware components of the computer. There are five key functions of an operating system:
- System supervision – manages memory, controls programs and processes
- Hardware services – control devices like the hard drive and monitor
- Software services – provide file system support and user interfaces
- Communication services – control communication with external systems or within the local network
- Security – controls access to the system and files

The **memory manager** is in charge of allocating RAM memory for a program to run in. Operating systems can support one of two types of memory management: **monoprogramming,** where only one program can run at a time, or **multiprogramming**, where one or more programs can reside in RAM memory and execute simultaneously. In multiprogramming, programs may not run exactly simultaneously but run concurrently with the operating system, allowing one program to run for a while and then switching to the other program.

There are several techniques for the operating system to achieve multiprogramming. One is by **partitioning**, where several programs are moved into a fixed area of RAM memory called a partition. In this scheme, the operating system alternates between the programs as already described. The other is **paging**. A program is divided into page segments; the advantage of paging is that the smaller page segments can be loaded into any available page in RAM memory. Think of pages as a large number of small partitions. Paging is flexible because partitioning requires a large amount of contiguous memory while paging allows the pages to be scattered. Paging is a form of **virtual memory** where parts of a program are stored on the hard disk. The term **thrashing** is used to describe the unusual condition of a program that requires the operating system to swap virtual memory pages inefficiently.

The **process manager** manages programs that are currently executing in memory, which are called **processes** in many operating system environments. A process typically executes in memory until it needs some input or output (I/O) function, for example, waiting for user input from the keyboard or writing data to the hard disk. Or it executes until it uses up the CPU time allocated to it by the operating system or until the process completes.

In the meantime, the **device manager** manages the access to the I/O devices. Another name for the device manager is the **I/O supervisor**. I/O devices are significantly slower than the speed of the CPU, so the process must wait until the I/O operation is complete before continuing to execute. The device manager monitors the device to assure that it is turned on and ready to process; it maintains a list or queue of processes that need to access the device, and it determines which processes access the device based upon priorities set in the operating system. Each device, such as a printer, needs a **device driver** which is a program that provides the operating system with the information it needs to work with the device.

A **spooler** is a program within the operating system that sends requests for printing on a printer to a file on disk rather than directly to the printer. The device manager thinks that it is printing to a very fast printer, but what is actually happening is that all the printed output is being collected on the hard disk to be printed as continuous pages at a later time. Otherwise, processes would be stalled as they waited while one process "hogged" the printer.

Some CPU's and their operating systems utilize the concept of an **interrupt** which is a signal to the CPU that a process needs to stop momentarily to process an I/O or some other type of request, including error interrupts. The **interrupt handler** is the program within the operating system that analyzes the interrupt signal to determine its type. If the signal is an I/O request the interrupt handler passes the request to the device manager or I/O supervisor.

There are several properties of operating systems that apply to how requested programs execute, and it is important to understand the different terms because they are easily confused:

- **Batch processing** – typical of mainframe computers with a large number of users; a program or series of programs are executed under the control of the operating system without interaction with a user. The user "submits" a batch request and the operating system schedules the execution based on priorities set by management; the user is informed when the task is complete. In a PC operating system, batch files have the suffix .BAT. Batch processing is suitable for tasks that are routine and periodic in nature that can wait until computer resources are available. Batch processing is efficient because all transactions of the same type are processed together.

- **Real-time** – immediate processing of transactions as they occur. Real-time systems are the same as online processing and require online random or direct access files.

- **Multiple program loading** – an operating system that lets the user start more than one program at a time; however, only one of the programs is active at a time.

- **Multiprocessing** – the simultaneous execution of different portions of a program by a multiprocessor, a computer with more than one CPU. This type of processing requires an operating system that is capable of parallel processing.
- **Multitasking** – the execution of more than one program at a time on a computer system; one task executes in the foreground and interfaces with the user. Another program that does not require interface with a user executes in the background. An example of a background task is printing spooled output while the user is on the Internet.
- **Multiprogramming** – same as multiple program loading.
- **Multithreading** – a form of multitasking where multiple tasks run under the same program. For example, one copy of a word processor might be used by several workstations at the same time.
- **Fault tolerant computing** – the ability of the system to produce correct results and continue processing even if hardware or software errors have occurred. This can be accomplished by redundant computer components that duplicate processing or error correcting memory.

The term **boot** is used to refer to the process required to clear RAM memory, load the operating system and prepare the computer for use. This term comes from the earliest days of computing. A **cold boot** occurs whenever the computer is powered on and a **warm boot** occurs when the user requests a system restart. An equivalent term for boot is **reboot.**

In addition to the operating system are **system support programs** that provide common useful functions, for example, produce a screen image or printout of the files on a hard disk. Such programs are called **system utilities**. As a group, these programs are known as **system software**.

 Software Development Methods & Tools

METHODS

One software development method is the traditional software or **systems development** which is an 8-step process required to construct an information system that addresses a particular problem, such as implementing an online reservation system. Synonymous terms are **information system development, application development,** or **waterfall model**.

A properly implemented information system development progresses through eight well-defined stages:

- **Systems investigation** – the feasibility stage where a go/no go evaluation is performed to determine if it is cost-effective to implement the system.
- **Feasibility studies** or preliminary studies that investigate the needs of prospective users, resource needs, costs and benefits of the new system are done during this stage.
- **Systems analysis** – the tasks are to define the business problem, gather information about the existing approach or system, and determine the functional requirements for the new system. The analysis stage defines what the system will do.
- **Systems design** – the tasks are to define how the system will accomplish the requirements. The output of this phase is a system specification that includes the definition of:
  - System inputs, outputs and user interfaces
  - Any hardware, software, networking, procedures and staff needed to implement the system
  - How the components are integrated and how transactions flow through the system
- **Programming** – translating the design into computer code using a programming language.
- **Testing** – testing the code to ascertain that it will produce the desired results for every case.
- **Implementation** – conversion of the old system to the new system.
- **Operation** – the new system is placed into use.
- **Maintenance** – after the system is placed into operation, previously undetected errors must be corrected, updates made to handle changing requirements, and minor improvements or upgrades added.

Another application method is prototyping. **Prototyping** focuses on end-user requirements without doing feasibility studies or writing a specification. Prototyping is most suitable for smaller applications or for developing the user-interface portion of a large application.

Rapid application development (RAD) employs **CASE (Computer-Assisted Software Engineering) tools** to automate many of the tasks in the traditional systems development model. CASE tools include diagramming tools, analysis tools, document storage tools, documentation generators, and code generators.

Object-oriented development also differs from the traditional systems development model in that the approach emphasizes the use of "objects" which are aspects of the real world that must be modeled by the application system rather than the step-by-step processing that is needed. An object-oriented approach to a billing application should be amenable to other mailings as well because the real-world functions are similar.

TOOLS

There are two traditional tools for managing the systems development. A **Gantt chart** shows the amount of time allocated for each step in the systems development process. Of course, in business, each of the eight steps is broken down into hundreds of finer-grained tasks so there are many Gantt charts used to allocate and track time.

Another type of chart that tracks time estimates is a **PERT (Program Evaluation and Review Techniques) chart** which shows the interrelationship of tasks as connected network nodes. A PERT chart is particularly useful for showing the dependency of tasks, that Task A must be complete before Task B can begin.

A **system flowchart** may be used during the systems design stage to illustrate in diagram form how the system is constructed in terms of files, processing, inputs and outputs. A commonly used set of symbols is employed when constructing any type of flowchart. The system flowchart typically emphasizes the physical devices that are used by the system. Detail level flowcharts that emphasize the logical structure of processing may also be constructed for every process in the system before programming begins. Similarly, a **data flow diagram** can show the logical relationship of data to the external entities like departments within the business.

PSEUDOCODE

After the system specification is complete but before the design is coded in the actual programming language, portions of the system may be coded in what is called **pseudocode,** a design technique that lays out the processing in a simple but standardized language so that the logic can be examined before it is translated into the more complex programming language.

Before delving into pseudocode, we must consider how expressions are processed in most computers. Expression processing uses concepts from algebra for computing the results of evaluating expressions. In most computer languages as well as in pseudocode, the normal symbols + for add, - for subtract, * for multiply, and / for divide are used. Exponentiation, or raising a number to a power, has various representations in the different languages, and for our discussion here we will use the symbol ** which is used in several languages and in pseudocode.

The expression A + B * C means to take the value of A, B, and C and perform the indicated operations. However, the rules of **operator precedence** apply when there are no parentheses in the expression. In the absence of parentheses the rule of operator precedence from highest precedence to lowest precedence is:

1) Any exponentiation is evaluated first
2) Followed by any multiplication or division in their order of appearance from left to right
3) Followed by any addition or subtraction in their order of appearance

So for our simple example, if A has the value 2, B is 3, and C is 4, the expression value is 3 * 4 + 2 which is 14.

However, if parentheses are added to the expression, expressions in parentheses are evaluated first, starting with innermost parentheses. Within parentheses, the above operator precedence rule still applies. If we rewrite our simple expression to (A + B) * C we now add A and B to get 5, then multiply by 4 to get 20.

Continuing to use the same values, A is 2, B is 3, and C is 4:

1) C – A ** 2 is 0
2) A + B * C ** 2 is 82
3) (A + B) * C ** 2 is 80
4) ((A + B) * C) ** 2 is 400

Pseudocode resembles English and contains the following simple statements which are sufficient to describe any process:

- **Sequence** – an ordered series of simple actions like computations. The pseudocode code statement is SET.

- **Decision branching** – tests a relationship in the process (called a condition) and performs one sequence if the relationship is true and a different sequence if the relationship is false. The pseudocode statement is
    IF (condition) … THEN…ELSE…END IF.

- **Repetition** – the order to continue to perform a sequence of actions while a condition is true. Skip to the sequence following the repetition when the condition becomes false. The pseudocode statement is WHILE (condition)…END WHILE.

A condition can be a comparison. Possible comparisons are:
    = tests if the two values are the same
    > tests if the left operand is greater than the right operand
    < tests if the left operand is smaller than the right operand
    >= tests if the left operand is greater than or equal to the right operand
    <= tests if the left operand is less than or equal to the right operand.

A condition can use **logical operators**. The logical operators are AND, OR and NOT.
- AND   is true if both of the operators are true and false otherwise
- OR   is true if either or both of the operators are true and false otherwise
- NOT   reverses the value of true to false and false to true

Again continuing to use the same values, A is 2, B is 3, and C is 4:
- A = B is false
- A > B is false
- A < B is true

The SET statement gives a value to a variable. Here is an example of a sequence of pseudocode instructions using only SET instructions:

    SET A TO 2

gives A the value of 2

    SET B TO 3
    SET C TO 4
    SET C TO A + B

changes C from 4 to 5

    SET A TO B * C

changes A from 2 to 15. Why? The previous SET statement changed the value of C. The statements are an example of a sequence of actions that, if they were written in a programming language, the computer would execute in order.

The IF…THEN…ELSE…END IF statement is a decision branching statement that tests the condition specified in the IF clause. If the condition is true, the sequence of statements in the THEN clause is executed and the sequence of statements in the ELSE clause is skipped. If the condition is false, the sequence of instructions in the THEN clause is skipped and the sequence of statements in the ELSE clause is executed. In either case, after the THEN or ELSE sequence, execution goes to the statement after the END IF. Using the values of A, B, and C from the last example,

    IF (A > B) THEN
    SET LARGER TO A
    ELSE
    SET LARGER TO B
    END IF
    SET A TO 0
    SET B TO 0

After this pseudocode is evaluated, what are the values of A, B, and LARGER? A started out as 15 and B was 3. Since 15 > 3 is true LARGER becomes 15, the ELSE clause is skipped and both A and B are set to zero. Which clause would be executed if

A and B were equal? The condition (A > B) would be false so the ELSE clause is the one that would be executed.

Repetition is coded as a WHILE loop in pseudocode. The following example showing a **WHILE loop** in pseudocode instructions is from the CLEP sample test.

```
SET A TO 1
SET B TO 3
SET A TO A + B
WHILE A < 20
SET A TO (A * A)/2
END WHILE
```

An important point about using a WHILE loop is that some statement within the WHILE and END WHILE pair must change a value in the condition that is being tested to eventually make the condition false, otherwise the loop will run forever. In the above pseudocode A has the value of 4 when the sequence of instructions reaches the WHILE statement for the first time. Since 4 is less than 20, the condition is true and the sequence of statements within the WHILE loop is executed. The value of A changes to 4 * 4 / 2 which is 8. The sequence encounters the END WHILE and repetition causes the execution to return to the WHILE statement. The value of A is still less than 20 so the WHILE sequence is entered once again. This time A is set to 8 * 8 / 2 which is 32. The END WHILE is processed and repetition causes the WHILE to be evaluated again. This time A is greater than 20 and the processing skips to the non-existent sequence after the END WHILE. For this example, the final value of A is 32.

Note that A, B, and C are just arbitrary names for the values. The name given to a value can be any letter or descriptive name like:
SET AREA TO LENGTH * WIDTH

CONVERSION TO A NEW SYSTEM

Most information systems today are replacing an older or out-of-date existing system. There are four methods for converting use of the old system to the new system. **Parallel conversion** means that both the old and the new system are used simultaneously and the results are compared periodically to detect errors. **Phased conversion** puts only a portion of the new system into use at one time or allows only certain departments to begin using the system. **Pilot conversion** means that only one department or physical location is the first to use and test the new system. **Plunge** is the term given to the abrupt changeover to a new system without using one of the other conversion techniques first.

 # Programming Languages

At the outset, the only programming language available was **machine language**, which was unique to each model of computer and was programmed in binary using only 0's and 1's. Machine language was quickly replaced by **symbolic language** that replaced the binary number for an instruction with a defined acronym. The first symbolic languages were **assembly languages** because the acronyms were "assembled" into strings of 0's and 1's. Assembly language is still in active use today for special purpose computer applications.

Using assembly language requires that every CPU instruction must be coded by the programmer; therefore, there is a one-to-one correspondence between a line of code in assembly language and a line of code in machine language. Assembly language has been superseded by **high level languages** that are independent of the instruction set of the CPU, resulting in code that can be executed on more than one model of CPU. High level languages are also an attempt to come closer to **natural language**, like English, when programming a computer.

With a high level language, the program must still be translated eventually into machine language for execution. After a program is written in a high level language, it is processed by another program called a **compiler,** which performs the necessary translation into machine language. Interpreters directly execute instructions written in a high level computer programming language. This is done by translating it into a language which the interpreter is able to execute instructions from. This is the main difference between the two. Compilers translate to machine language that the computer understands, and the interpreter translates to languages which it understands. Of the two, compilers are more common.

CATEGORIES OF HIGH LEVEL LANGUAGES

Today, there are five categories of high level languages. The categories are listed below with examples of each type.

- **Procedural** – a set of instructions that are executed in the order indicated
  - **FORTRAN** (Formula Translation) – early language available in 1957; ideal for scientific and engineering applications even today.
  - **BASIC** (Beginner's All-Purpose Symbolic Instruction Code) – developed in 1964 for teaching purposes; resurrected in the 1990's for use on personal computers because BASIC does not require a compiler.
  - **COBOL** (Common Business-Oriented Language) – available in the early 1960's for business applications; still in active use today. **Pascal** – available in the 1970's as a language for teaching students.
  - **C language** – also available in the early 1970's and developed for writing the UNIX operating system. Gained popularity as a general purpose language for implementing other kinds of systems.

- **Object-oriented** – the programmer defines objects and the operations for each object
  - **C++** – has three main principles: **1) encapsulation** or hiding the data inside the object; **2) inheritance** whereby an object can inherit properties from another object; and **3) polymorphism** that allows the programmer to define multiple operations with the same name that do different processing in different classes. C++ is a general-purpose language based upon C.
  - **Java** – based upon both C and C++. A program in Java can be either an application or an **applet**, a mini-program that is embedded in a web document and executed by a browser after downloading. A **servlet** is an applet that runs on a server. Note: **JavaScript** was developed by Netscape to allow Java-like programming but it is not related to the Java language. JavaScript was created by a completely different company than Java and functions differently as well. While Java creates independent programs, JavaScript must be placed inside an HTML document. It is less complex than Java and is used to make a webpage more interactive than basic HTML can.

- **Functional** – defines a set of primitive functions and allows the programmer to combine these to create new functions. Functional languages are not used to implement information systems.
  - **Lisp** – defined in the early 1960's.

- **Declarative** – based on formal logic. Declarative languages are not used to implement information systems.

- **Prolog** – defined in the early 1970's.

- **Special** – new languages that do not fit in the four traditional categories.
  - **HTML** (HyperText Markup Language) – is not a real programming language but it allows formatting instructions to be embedded in a file. The user's web browser interprets the formatting instructions when the file is displayed on the user's monitor. The file is composed of the text and formatting **tags** that are enclosed in angle brackets (< >). An HTML name and its parameters occur within the brackets. An HTML program is composed of a head and a body. The head contains the title and other browser parameters. The body contains the text and the formatting tags.
  - **PERL** (Practical Extraction and Report Language) – It is used in web development, data analysis and web applications. It was designed to test web applications written in any language, making it useful. It also works well for creating, expanding or enhancing games or graphics. It is similar to C but adds the capability to scan text files, extract information from the text, and prepare a report from the information. PERL is in active use to create Common Gateway Interface (CGI) scripts that handle the output of HTML forms. PERL may also be called a **scripting language** as is JavaScript because they are used to produce a **script** or series of instructions that tells a program how to perform a specific procedure.
  - **SQL** (Structured Query Language) – a language that is used to interrogate a database.

CGI INTERFACE

CGI stands for Common Graphics Interface. CGI is not a separate programming language. It is an interface used to create interactive elements. For example, this is used with online surveys. Based on the information you put into the form on the first page, it will ask you different questions on the second page. Or, if a web page with a map and you click on different parts of the map, different information is displayed. For these types of programs to work, the browser and server have to communicate back and forth dependent on your responses. CGI allows this to happen. CGI can be written in many different languages, but most commonly PERL is used.

User Interfaces

Today's interactive software relies heavily on the **graphical user interface (GUI)** which uses symbols to represent program or computer functions. These symbols are called **icons**. The GUI became popular after a team of researchers at Xerox Corporations found that people recognize graphic representations faster than they can read words or phrases. GUI's typically are comprised of pull-down menus, dialog boxes, check boxes, radio buttons, drop-down list boxes, scrollbars, navigational bars and the like. Programs that use GUI require more powerful computers with a sophisticated display monitor.

Before Windows, users communicated with their computers through command prompts in DOS. A command line could be something like: d://open newdoc.txt

User interfaces must take into account the human being who is the intended user of the information system. **Ergonomics**, the science of designing machines, computers, and physical work areas so that people find them easy to use, is an important consideration in the design of GUI's. Making a start button pink and a stop button yellow goes against lifelong training that green means go and red means stop and is not an ergonomically sound design choice.

Presentation graphics are designed to present information in graphical form, like line or bar graphs or pie charts, that helps illustrate trends and relationships in the data in order to help managers and users make better informed decisions. This type of information is easier to grasp in a visual rather than numeric format.

Multimedia presentations integrate multiple media like text, graphics, voice, and other sounds, and photographs and video clips are gaining in popularity as well. Hypermedia is the term given to a hypertext system that uses multimedia resources. Hypertext is a method of preparing and publishing text so that the user can select their own path through the material. Hyperlinks, which are underlined words or phrases, display another page of information when the user clicks on the link with a mouse. This type of user interface leaves users in complete control of how they navigate the information rather than being forced to view the information sequentially in the order established by someone else.

Interactive video systems combine image processing with text, audio, and video capabilities. Software exists to produce these interactive digital video (DVI) applications.

Software Packages

Software applications can be divided into two classes:

- **Proprietary** – an information processing application that was developed by staff in a particular company or contracted with a software development company for use solely by the company.
- **Off-the-shelf or package** – software designed for general use that can be purchased or leased from a software vendor.

There are numerous familiar types of software packages such as:

- **Data management software** – supports potentially massive database files.
- **Word processing** – supports production of documents; examples are Microsoft Word and Corel WordPerfect.
- **Desktop publishing** – incorporates photographs, diagrams, and other images with text to produce sophisticated documents equivalent to those produced at a printing house. Professionals use programs such as Quark Express or Adobe InDesign for layout and publishing. Adobe Illustrator and Adobe Photoshop are two other programs used to create or modify graphics which are later imported to a Desktop publishing program.
- **Graphics software** – allows the user to convert data to a graphical form.
- **Presentation graphics software** – typically contains drawing tools and other presentation aids for creating professional-looking audience presentations. Examples include Microsoft PowerPoint and Presentations.
- **Analysis graphics** – graphically represents data that has been analyzed statistically.
- **Spreadsheet software** – most commonly used is Microsoft Excel.
- **CAD (Computer-Aided Design) software** – supports advanced engineering design.
- **Multimedia software** – handles multiple media for input or output of data, particularly the combination of spatial-based media like text and images with time-based media like sound and video.
- **Interactive multimedia software** – allows the user to control the flow of information; used in museums and information kiosks.
- **Communications software** – supports interconnection of computers. Network operating systems are an example of a sophisticated communications software package.

- **Speech recognition software** – software that provides for recognition of human speech in real-time.
- **Decision support system (DSS)** – software that aids in management decision making.
- **Groupware** – software that promotes communication and collaboration among a group of people who are typically co-workers.
- **Software suite** – a collection of related software packages from the same vendor that are bundled together at one price.
- **Multimedia and web design** – programs used to develop websites, HTML documents and emails as well as Flash promotions. Macromedia Flash, Macromedia Dreamweaver and Microsoft FrontPage are all examples.

 Software Development

There are six main stages to the software development life cycle:

1. Analysis – determining if the software is a viable product and/or can it be created.
2. Design – designing the layout of the software.
3. Development – creating of the software.
4. Debugging – when the software appears complete, developers will test it themselves to find the bugs or problems with the program.
5. Testing – once the developers have tested it extensively and cannot find any additional bugs, they may release the software to a small group called beta testers. Sometimes these testers are individuals outside the company. These testers are also sometimes customers who begin to use the product as they normally would and when they come across a problem, they notify the developers.
6. Maintenance – once software is released to the general public for sale, sometimes there are additional issues not caught by the testers or developers. When these problems are significant, the software company will issue a patch or service pack that must be installed to fix these issues.

Data Management

HYPERTEXT AND HYPERMEDIA

Hypertext and hypermedia are revolutionary concepts transforming how we interact with and consume information in the digital age. Hypertext is a methodology that allows for the interactive reading of documents stored in a text database. It enables users to navigate the document by clicking on hyperlinks, embedded references that connect related pieces of information. This non-linear approach to reading allows users to explore the document in a way that suits their interests and needs rather than following a predetermined sequence.

Hypertext documents typically contain text and a limited number of graphics, such as images and diagrams. The hyperlinks within the document can lead to other sections of the same document or to external sources, providing a seamless and interconnected reading experience. Software packages like Adobe Acrobat and Microsoft Word have built-in features for creating hypertext documents, making it easier for authors to incorporate hyperlinks and create interactive content.

Hypermedia, on the other hand, takes the concept of hypertext a step further by incorporating multiple forms of media, including text, graphics, audio, and video. This allows for a more immersive and engaging experience, as users can interact with various types of content within a single document. For example, a hypermedia document about a historical event might include text descriptions, images of relevant artifacts, audio recordings of eyewitness accounts, and video clips of reenactments or documentaries.

The combination of hypertext and hypermedia has given rise to electronic books or e-books. E-books are digital versions of traditional printed books that can be read on electronic devices such as smartphones, tablets, and dedicated e-readers like Amazon Kindle or Kobo. They offer several advantages over physical books, including portability, searchability, and the ability to include interactive elements like hyperlinks and multimedia content.

One notable example of a hypermedia e-book is "Our Choice" by Al Gore, which explores the topic of climate change. The e-book features interactive graphics, animations, and documentary videos that enhance the reading experience and provide a deeper understanding of the subject matter. Another example is "The Wasteland" by T.S. Eliot, which has been adapted into a hypermedia edition that includes audio recordings of the poem, annotations, and scholarly commentary.

The educational sector has also embraced hypertext and hypermedia, with many textbooks and learning materials now available in digital formats. For instance, "Principles of Biology" by Nature Education is an interactive online textbook incorporating hyperlinks, animations, and quizzes to engage students and reinforce key concepts.

As technology continues to advance, the possibilities for hypertext and hypermedia are expanding. With the increasing availability of virtual and augmented reality devices, we can expect to see even more immersive and interactive forms of electronic books in the future. The integration of hypertext and hypermedia has revolutionized how we consume and interact with information, providing a more dynamic and personalized reading experience.

DATABASE MANAGEMENT SYSTEMS

A database management system goes beyond the capabilities of the original file systems and allows the definition, creation, and maintenance of a database. A database is a collection of related information about a particular subject organized in such a way as to facilitate retrieval and update. A database management system (DBMS) is a set of computer programs that controls the creation, maintenance, and use of an organization's databases. A DBMS facilitates data organization by providing sorting and grouping options for reports. The data dictionary is a database of all the names and descriptions of all types of data records and their interrelationships.

A database management system is designed based upon one of several database data models: hierarchical, network, relational, distributed, object-oriented, or hypermedia. In the hierarchical model, which is obsolete in today's technology, data is stored as an upside-down tree structure with a root at the highest level and data stored down the branches. It is an example of a one-to-many relationship among the records because one root has many branches.

The network model can represent more complicated data with many-to-many relationships. The data is organized like a hierarchy, but information at any level can point to multiple pieces of information at a subordinate level. Network models are also obsolete.

Today, database management systems are based upon the relational model, which makes the data appear as a relation, a two-dimensional table. Note that this is not how the data is actually stored on the hard disk. Every relation in the database has a name and one or more attributes, where the attributes define the columns of the table. Each column of the table defines a distinct data element.

The distributed model is simply a relational model where the data is distributed over one or more computers that may or may not be in the same physical location. The object-oriented model is related to object-oriented programming and consists of objects, attributes, classes, methods, and messages. In a hypermedia or hypertext model, the relationships between data elements are less structured than in a traditional database because the elements define text, graphics, sound, or full-motion video.

A database management system supports organizing and retrieving the data in sorted or grouped order for reporting purposes. Structured query language (SQL) is used to interrogate the database and retrieve groups of records for analysis.

A **data warehouse** is a relational database management system that is designed to support management decision-making. Data is usually stored differently in the warehouse than in the operational database. A **data mart** is a smaller version of a data warehouse that focuses on one subject area. **Data mining** provides a mechanism for extracting previously unknown trends or forecasts from the data in a data warehouse or data mart.

There are many advantages to using a database management system. The DBMS, especially through use of the data dictionary, promotes the standardization of data. The DBMS consolidates the data so that it does not need to be duplicated and stored in many files across the organization. Rather than needing many different programs to process the data, all data access is done through the DBMS. Data is accessible and shared among all users and a common security system to protect data is in place.

DATA CONCEPTS AND DATA STRUCTURES

The simple pseudocode language that was introduced earlier relied solely on the concept of a simple **variable**, a single location in memory that can store just one value. From the almost absurd examples of pseudocode, it is easy to see that programming with just variables is not particularly useful. The power of information systems lies in their ability to process vast quantities of similar information, like all customers, all inventory or all suppliers.

A **data structure** defines a collection of related variables that can be processed either individually or as a whole. Procedural programming languages support some advanced data structures but the latest database management systems are needed for handling much of the real-time processing that occurs today.

Procedural languages like FORTAN and COBOL use a data structure called an array for storing items in a list. Think of an array like a grocery shopping list where every item on the list can be found in one grocery store. An **array** is a fixed-size sequenced collection of elements all having the same data type. A **data type** defines what kind of values can be stored in a variable or other data structure element, such as integer or text. A **subscript** is used to select which element of the array to process, where the subscript is usually a simple variable like the A, B or C in the examples that is incremented by one as it steps through the elements of the array. The grocery list is an example of a **one-dimensional array** and a table with rows and columns is a **two-dimensional array.** Arrays are always stored in the computer's memory when the program is running.

A **record** is a collection of related elements, usually with different data types. A record is given a record name and each element in the record is called a **field**. An example of a record is customer data with a name, address, and dollar amount owed. Records are stored in files on the hard disk and must be read and rewritten in order to be processed.

Procedural languages can process two types of files: sequential and random. A **sequential file** must be read from disk from beginning to end. In order to process any record, the entire file before it must be read. Sequential files are useful when all of the data items must be processed on a routine basis. In a **random file,** any record can be accessed as long as the **record key**, for example, the customer account number, is known. Historically, sequential and random files were used primarily in batch processing mainframe systems. A random file can also be called a **direct access file**.

DOCUMENT IMAGES

Image processing has revolutionized the way we handle documents. It enables the electronic capture, storage, processing, and retrieval of document images containing various types of content, such as numeric data, typed text, handwriting, graphics, and photographs. This technology has found widespread applications in industries ranging from healthcare and finance to legal services and government institutions.

One example of image processing in action is the digitization of medical records. Healthcare providers can scan patient files, including handwritten notes, test results, and X-ray images, and store them electronically. This allows for quick and easy access to patient information, streamlining the healthcare process and improving patient care.

Similarly, financial institutions use image processing to digitize and process checks, loan applications, and other financial documents. By automating these processes, banks can reduce errors, improve efficiency, and provide faster customer service.

Electronic Document Management (EDM) systems take image processing further by integrating additional features and functionalities. These systems not only handle document images but can also incorporate voice messages, word processors, and desktop publishing tools. For instance, a law firm might use an EDM system to manage case files, including scanned legal documents, recorded depositions, and electronically drafted contracts.

Another example of an EDM system is a content management system (CMS) used by a publishing company. The CMS allows authors to submit their work electronically, editors to collaborate on revisions, and designers to create layouts using desktop publishing tools. The final product, such as a magazine or book, can be stored and distributed electronically.

The integration of image processing and EDM systems has greatly enhanced our ability to manage and access information, making document-intensive processes more efficient and cost-effective. As technology advances, we can expect to see even more sophisticated applications of these tools in various industries.

UNITS OF MEASUREMENT

A **kilobyte** is a unit of measurement for disk space, memory, etc. A kilobyte equals 1000 bytes. The actual value of a kilobyte is 1024. Megabyte equals 1 million bytes or 1000 kilobytes. Megahertz or **MHz** represents 1 million cycles a second. MHz is used to measure speed in buses and microprocessors. A **baud** is the rate a file is transferred, i.e., 200 baud = 200 bits per second. Another transfer rate is BPS, or bits per second.

FILE NAMES

The guidelines for naming Windows documents are fairly open, but there are nine symbols which may not be used. These symbols are greater than signs (>), less than signs (<), colons (:), quotation marks ("), backslashes (\), forward slashes (/), absolute value signs (|), question marks (?), and asterisks (*). Also, the path name for a document, which includes information describing where the document is found, can be no longer than 260 characters.

Information Processing Management

SYSTEM DEVELOPMENT PROCESSES

Developing a business solution using computers is called information systems or application development. The major activities are investigation, analysis, design, implementation, and maintenance. Together, this is called the information systems development cycle or the life cycle of the system.

The investigation phase may be called information systems planning. Strategic planning deals with policies, strategies, and objectives that meet the information needs of the entire organization. Operational planning deals with operating budgets, including budgets for information systems maintenance, upgrades, and new projects. Project planning is the first step in developing a new information system and is the first step in the waterfall software development model already discussed.

Part of planning is conducting feasibility studies. A cost/benefit analysis projects the system's costs and potential long-term savings. Economic feasibility takes the cost/benefit analysis results to determine if the project should continue. Technical feasibility determines if the proposed project can actually be accomplished with currently available technology. Operational feasibility determines if management and employees can utilize the new system effectively.

The activities of information system development overlap in time. For example, it doesn't matter whether you call the feasibility studies part of the system development or part of the software development. In a particular organization, the difference is primarily in the title of the staff that performs the studies.

TYPES OF INFORMATION PROCESSING APPLICATIONS

Central to any business is the concept of a transaction and a **transaction processing system (TPS)** supports the need of a business to track transactions such as order processing, general ledger, accounts payable and receivable, inventory management, payroll, and data required by law.

Batch processing is not interactive and has its roots in the original mainframe environment of the 1960's. A batch application gathers information over a period of time and records the individual transactions in a file. At routine time intervals (daily, weekly), the file of accumulated transactions is processed against a **master file** that contains the status of each account, for example. The entire set of transactions is processed, resulting in the update of the entire master file during one batch processing session. A primary concept of batch processing is sorted order. The master file records are stored with a key, like an account number, that is sorted in ascending or descending order. The transaction file is then also sorted into the same order so that the transactions and master records can more easily be matched together. The major disadvantage of batch processing is that the master file is out-of-date between updates and it not responsive to the real-time needs of inquiries.

Real-time processing means that transactions are processed immediately. The familiar **online transaction processing (OLTP)** systems are an example of real-time processing. Files and databases are always up-to-date and no sorting is required. However, additional security and error detection software must be added to real-time systems to prevent instantaneous corruption of the data.

STANDARDS

The world cannot function without standards and the information processing industry is no exception. There are numerous professional and governmental agencies that cooperate to standardize programming languages. For example, the Conference on Data-Systems Languages (**CODASYL**) is the professional organization that is responsible for improving and standardizing COBOL. The **American National Standards Institute (ANSI)** develops standards for all the major programming languages. Groups such as the Internet Engineering Task Force and the World Wide Web Consortium have defined standards for the Internet.

 Security and Controls

There are three types of controls for ensuring the security of an information system: information system controls, procedural controls, and physical facility controls.

Information system controls attempt to ensure the accuracy of data and results. **Garbage in/garbage out (GIGO)** means when invalid data is entered the results will also be invalid. Error checking of keyed inputs for range of values and other characteristics or only allowing selections from drop-down input boxes prevents invalid data from entering the system. An **audit trail** provides for tracing the entire processing path of a transaction.

Encryption of data, modifying it so that it cannot be deciphered with the encryption key, is a key method of securing transmitted data. **Decryption** is the restoration of the message to its original form. Data that is not encrypted is called **plaintext** while data that is encrypted is called **ciphertext**. The primary method in use today for data encryption is called **data encryption standard (DES)** which is a secret key form of encryption using one key. **Public key encryption** uses two keys: a **public key** that is broadcast and a **private key** that is known to the receiver of the data. Only the receiver can decrypt the message using the private key. The most common public key method is **Rivest-Shamir-Adleman (RSA) encryption**. A **digital signature** is a means of using public key encryption to verify the identity of a sender.

Procedural controls indicate how the operations should be conducted for maximum security. Separation of duties implies that one person does not have sufficient access to the system to corrupt it. Standardized procedures ensure and promote uniformity and guard against errors and fraud.

Verifying that a person who is attempting to access a computer system is an authorized user is an important procedural control and is called **authentication**. The main method used for authentication is the use of a **password**, a series of letters and numbers that presumably are known only between the system and the authorized user. The term **password protection** or **password protected** applies to the system itself, meaning that a password is required to access the system. Individuals who gain unauthorized access to a computer system are called **hackers. Biometric controls** which measure physical traits of a user such as retina or face scanning are becoming popular. Networks can be made more secure by the addition of a **firewall**, which protects the identity of the network nodes from the outside world of the Internet.

Physical facility controls are methods for protecting the physical plant from damage. Examples are: fire detection systems, emergency power systems, and temperature and humidity controls. Natural disasters do occur and every organization needs a **disaster recovery plan** which lays out responsibilities and procedures for continuing operations in the event of a disaster. A disaster recovery plan is not the same as a **system recovery plan** which provides for recovering from a major failure of the information processing system.

Personal computers that interact with other computers through a network or electronic mail can be subjected to attack by malicious programs. A **virus** is a program that embeds itself into another program and infects a personal computer when the other program runs. A virus will make copies of itself within other programs as well. A **worm** is a virus that will locate and corrupt data. A **Trojan horse** is a program that when installed contains unanticipated code that allows unauthorized collection or destruction of a user's data. The best protection from infection is to periodically run **virus-checking software** that will detect and eliminate known viruses.

Information Processing Careers

The following lists some of the career opportunities available in the information processing realm:
- Chief Information Officer (CIO) – executive director of information systems.
- Operations manager – in charge of the physical operation of computer equipment.
- Computer operator – person who is in charge of overseeing the daily activity of the computers.
- Network manager – in charge of computer network.
- Network specialist or network engineer – a person whose responsibility is to set up and maintain a network.
- Programming manager – in charge of programming activities.
- Analyst – in charge of analysis phases of system or software development and may perform design as well.
- Programmer – person who translates the design into code, performs testing (**debugging**, which is removal of errors), and documents the system components.

- Applications programmer – programmer whose job is to develop information systems or application programs.
- Systems programmer – a person who develops, sets up or maintains operating systems.
- Database programmer – a programmer whose specialty is programming interfaces to a data base management system.
- Database administrator (DBA) – person who defines and maintains a database and the data dictionary.

The titles given to individuals who work in information technology (IT) are as varied as the industries that employ them. The above is a sampling of some of the most popular titles.

 Applications in Organizations

MANAGEMENT DECISION MAKING

Business managers must decide about their areas of responsibility within the organization. Information applications can provide tools to aid the decision-making process, in addition to providing data in a report or graphical form. Analytical processing applications support decision-making by providing projections, comparisons, statistical inferences, and decision-analysis tools. A decision support system (DSS) and an executive information system (EIS) are examples of analytical applications.

These applications comprise data management, user interface, and model management. A DSS or EIS is based on a specialized database constructed for data mining. The user interface provides for interactive ad-hoc queries to the database, emphasizing graphical outputs. A model is a computer simulation based on mathematics or statistics of the real world. In a DSS or EIS, changing values within the model reflect the user's concept of changes in the real world to analyze "what-if" scenarios.

A geographic information system (GIS) integrates a geographic database with the DSS to accomplish analyses, for example, by geographic region. A GIS is capable of producing graphical outputs that contain maps. A GIS may be integrated with a global positioning system (GPS), which can pinpoint the unit's location being tracked anywhere in the world. A group decision support system (GDSS) supports exchanging ideas and opinions within a group or at a meeting. This may include an electronic meeting system (EMS).

A knowledge-based information system adds methods from artificial intelligence (AI), a branch of computer science that attempts to endow computers with the ability to make inferences from multiple hypotheses. An expert system is an application developed using AI methods applied to a highly specific area of knowledge and capable of giving advice about that area. Expert systems generate answers to questions in their area of expertise and can explain the rationale for the answer while performing the problem-solving work.

USER APPLICATIONS

Word processing software allows the user to create, edit, revise and print text material and to produce documents. These applications provide an editor for working on the text, a formatting program for producing documents, a dictionary, a thesaurus, a spelling and grammar checker, integrated graphics and a mail-merge capability. **Desktop publishing software** provides the next level of sophistication in supporting the layout of newsletters, announcements, and advertising copy.

Spreadsheet software allows the user to create a traditional spreadsheet or grid of rows and columns that can be tallied automatically and formatted in to reports or viewed graphically. Each grid entry is called a **cell**. Spreadsheet packages offer capabilities that facilitate what-if processing.

Graphics software supports the production of graphs, maps and drawings. **Presentation graphics software** contains presentation templates, multiple fonts, drawing tools, spelling checker, and possibly a library of clip art.

Speech recognition software recognizes human voice messages. **Discrete speech recognition** can recognize only one word at a time while **continuous speech recognition** recognizes normal speaking. Programs come with vocabularies of 30,000 to 75,000 words.

OFFICE SYSTEMS

Electronic mail (E-mail) sends and receives messages through a network. Users receive their messages after they log on to the network. An e-mail message can be broadcast to multiple users or an entire mailing list. Voice mail stores digitized voice messages. Facsimile (fax) capabilities can be integrated into personal computers, sending a message from the computer to any fax machine.

Electronic meeting systems (EMS) allow meetings and conferences to be held when participants are located in different physical locations. Teleconferencing is an electronic meeting supported by closed-circuit television broadcasting.

The above applications are components of office automation systems. These systems improve productivity by streamlining the flow of documents and messages among co-workers. Workgroup computing supports cooperative work. Other terms for workgroup computing are computer-supported collaboration (CSC), computer-based systems for collaborative work (CSCW), or collaborative work support systems (CWSS). People working together do not need to be in the same physical location. It is advantageous for the group to use the same suite of support programs because the bundling of software applications lowers the cost of purchase; programs in the suite work together; data and procedures can easily be shared amongst users while the organization maximizes its investment by using the full functionality of the suite.

Internet and the World Wide Web

The Internet is a network of computer networks. It originated in ARPANET, a U.S. Department of Defense network that began in 1969. ARPANET stands for Advanced Research Projects Agency Network. It was a wide-area network set up by the Department of Defense, which played an integral part in developing Internet protocols, although it was not technically the first Internet. Specifically, ARPANET developed the technology of packet switching, which, in part, allows the Internet to work efficiently and quickly.

The Internet comprises Internet service providers (ISPs) that typically provide network services to end-users for a monthly fee. Some ISPs are backbone networks that exist solely to connect the major networks of the other service providers.

Information on the Internet is transmitted as packets. A packet contains the information's sending and receiving addresses and sequence within the message. Individual packets comprising a message may take different routes over the network to the receiving computer, and the message is reassembled when all the packets arrive.

For example, when you send an email, the computer breaks it down into packets, each containing part of the information, such as the destination or the actual information of the email. The packets make their way to the correct place and then are reassembled. Packets are also used when downloading a file or a program. The program arrives in packets.

The protocol or standardized set of rules for transmitting packets is called Internet protocol (IP). Transport control protocol (TCP) is another protocol used in conjunction with IP. Taken together, these protocols are known as the TCP/IP protocol.

Every computer that accesses the Internet is given an IP address, which is four sets of numbers separated by dots, for example, 153.26.128.19. In addition, commercially used computers can have a domain name, which is more like natural language. The domain name begins with www. and may have multiple parts separated by dots.

However, standards exist for what the final part means, and the most prevalent suffixes are as follows: .com for commercial sites, .edu for educational sites, .mil for military sites, .gov for government sites, and .org for organizations or associations.

The Internet provides three main services: communication services such as electronic mail using simple mail transfer protocol (SMTP), newsgroups, chat rooms, and Internet telephone service; information retrieval services like gopher and file transfer protocol (FTP); and the World Wide Web (WWW). Another type of communication service is streaming audio and video that allows the user to hear and see the information as it is transmitted instead of waiting for packets to arrive. Numerous information retrieval services are available through the Internet.

File transfer protocol (FTP) provides access to a remote computer for retrieval of files. FTP stands for File Transfer Protocol. It is like HTTP, but used a little differently. While HTTP is used for viewing and updating web pages, FTP involves file transfers between computers. FTP is most often used by website designers and HTTP is used by Internet users. Like HTTP, when using FTP a person types in ftp://.

TCP/IP stands for Transmission Control Protocol/Internet Protocol. TCP/IP is the basic protocol used for sending information over the Internet. The first layer, TCP, is responsible for breaking the file or message into packets, which the receiving computer's TCP will reassemble. The second layer, IP, is responsible for telling each packet where to go.

Archie is a software tool that allows a user to search for files at a remote computer. A **gopher** is another software tool that allows users to locate other linked gopher files on Internet servers; users move from site to site searching for information at will. **Electronic Data Interchange (EDI)** is a standard for the electronic exchange of business documents such as invoices and purchase orders.

The World Wide Web is not the same as the Internet. The Internet is the network that transports packets while the World Wide Web is a computer application (software) that uses the network. Another application that uses the Internet is electronic mail. Anyone wishing to offer information through the World Wide Web must establish a **home page** on their **web site**. Every web site is identified by a **uniform resource locator (URL)**. Most URL's begin with **HTTP** which stands for **hypertext transfer protocol**, the transfer protocol for defining how messages are formatted and transmitted on the Web. The URL specifies the domain name of the web site possibly followed by the page identifier within the web site.

HTML stands for HyperText Markup Language. HTML is the computer programming language which is used in creating web pages. It uses a series of commands which the computer interprets as instructions for display of the web page. For example,

indicates a hard return in a line of text. The more complex the operation is, the more complex the code will be.

To create a simple list, several steps must be taken. First the list must be opened, <ul>, and each line must be started <li> and finished </li>. Then the list must be ended </ul>. Because creating HTML code by hand can become tedious and difficult, different languages and programs have been created to speed up the process.

HTTP stands for HyperText Transfer Protocol. It is the protocol for how servers and computers communicate. For example, a person types in http:// and the desired webpage, and the computer understands this to mean that the person wishes to see the web page. Literally, the browser sends a HTTP command to the server requesting the page. HTTP is mostly used as the protocol for Internet users wanting to view web pages.

A **browser** or **web browser** is a program that allows the user to navigate the World Wide Web. **Surfing** is the term given to exploring the links on the web in search of interesting information. A **search engine** is a program that allows the user to enter a word or phrase and the software returns a list of links to web sites that contain that word or phrase. Search engines locate web pages through registration, whereby the creator of the web site informs the search engine of its existence or through the use of a web crawler. A **web crawler** is an application that traverses the web automatically collecting links to be used later by the search engine. A **metasearch engine** submits a query to multiple search engines simultaneously.

The term IP address stands for Internet Protocol address. Every computer has its IP address, which identifies it and conveys that the computer follows the protocols and regulations for Internet communication and data transfers.

The term ISP stands for Internet Service Provider. An ISP is any company that offers Internet access in exchange for a periodic (usually monthly) fee.

The term URL stands for Uniform Resource Locator. This is often called the website address and is the information the computer uses to find a specific website.

As computers and the Internet become increasingly available and popular, several security problems develop. One such problem is hacking. Hacking is intentionally gaining access to a computer without the owner's permission or knowledge. Hacking is not necessarily always malicious. Often, people try to get into systems because they want to challenge themselves or think it will be fun. Also, companies will sometimes hire people to hack into their systems to find where the weaknesses in their security are. The term hacker is often used to refer to someone with malicious intentions who gains access to another person's computer.

Phishing and pharming are two different processes used by computer hackers to gain personal information about users. Phishing is when a person sends an e-mail that leads people to a site that looks legitimate and asks them to enter personal information. Pharming is when a hacker makes it so that when you try to go to a website, it is secretly automatically redirected to another fake website. Hackers can match the appearance and address of the site you mean to go to and use it to steal personal information.

Spoofing is the term for altering or obscured identity. One way is IP spoofing, which is when a person makes it appear that a message is coming from a different computer by altering the IP address. E-mail spoofing is when a person makes it appear that a message is coming from a different e-mail address than it is.

Spam is information, generally e-mails, sent indiscriminately to large numbers of people without their request or consent. Large-scale spamming can become a nuisance as it consumes a large portion of the network's bandwidth, slowing the Internet down, and wasting Internet users' time sorting through it. Sending obscene or abusive e-mails is called flaming.

Malware is software which is intended to damage or harm a computer. For example, viruses are malware. A virus is a piece of software which can attach itself to a file or program, and be passed from computer to computer as the file is opened. Viruses are generally attached to files which the computer user must click on (executable files), and therefore cannot spread without human action. Some viruses are activated when a computer turns on. A harmless virus may simply cause multiple pop-ups, but malicious viruses can alter programs, steal information or harm the computer. One type of virus is a Trojan horse. A Trojan horse is a program which appears useful to the computer user, but either before, after or during installation, it steals information or harms the computer in some way.

Another type of virus is a worm. Worms are a type of virus which do not require human action to travel. They spread from computer to computer using information on a person's computer. For example, a virus attached to an e-mail which automatically sends itself to everyone on a person's contact list would be a worm.

Firewalls and antivirus software are two types of programs which help protect the computer from viruses. A firewall is basically a barrier between your computer and other computers. It scans incoming data to be sure it meets security requirements and protects against hackers. While firewalls deal mainly with incoming information, antivirus software scans the programs already on the computer for anything dangerous.

 Zombie and Slave Computers

The terms zombie computer and slave computer both refer to methods of computer control. However, slave computers involve voluntary and helpful computer control, and zombie computers involve involuntary and illegal computer control. The terms "zombie computer" and "slave computer" refer to computers that have been compromised and are under the control of a malicious actor, often without the knowledge of the legitimate owner. These compromised machines are then used to conduct various nefarious activities, such as distributed denial-of-service (DDoS) attacks, email spam campaigns, and cryptocurrency mining.

From a technical perspective, a computer becomes a zombie or slave when infected with malware that allows remote control by an attacker. This malware can be introduced through various means, such as phishing emails, infected websites, or unpatched software vulnerabilities. Once the malware is installed, it establishes a connection with a command-and-control (C&C) server, which the attacker controls. The C&C server can then issue commands to the compromised machine, directing it to perform specific tasks or join a botnet, a network of infected computers working together under the attacker's control.

The implications of zombie and slave computers can be severe. Botnets composed of these compromised machines can be used to launch large-scale DDoS attacks, which can overwhelm targeted websites or networks, rendering them inaccessible to legitimate users. This can lead to significant financial losses for businesses and disrupt critical services. Additionally, these botnets can be used to distribute spam emails, which not only clutter inboxes but can also spread further malware or conduct phishing attempts.

Another concern is the unauthorized use of compromised computers' resources, such as processing power and bandwidth. Attackers may use zombie computers to mine cryptocurrencies, taking advantage of the collective computing power to generate profits while leaving the legitimate owners to bear the costs of increased electricity consumption and hardware wear and tear.

Maintaining proper cybersecurity practices is essential to mitigate the risk of falling victim to these threats. This includes keeping operating systems and software up to date with the latest security patches, using reputable antivirus and anti-malware software, and educating users about safe browsing habits and the dangers of phishing attempts. Additionally, implementing network security measures, such as firewalls and intrusion detection systems, can help detect and prevent unauthorized access to computers and networks.

Email

Netiquette is the etiquette of the Internet. It is a set of guidelines dictating what it is or isn't proper to do online. For example, typing in all capitals is inappropriate because it indicates yelling. Netiquette also includes practices such as not publishing other people's e-mail addresses without their permission and never forwarding a message without reading it first. Mass forwarding is also discouraged. Messages should only be sent to the necessary recipients. Also, accurate and descriptive subjects should be used. Proper netiquette does allow for the use of emoticons (series of characters representative of facial expressions) where appropriate. Common sense is the rule for online interaction. If you wouldn't do or say something in real life, then don't say it on the Internet.

History of Computing

Computing was created when humans began using more and more complex math. Beginning by counting on his fingers, man progressed from notches in bones to the use of the abacus and the personal calculator.

Need once again proves to be the mother of invention. Humans cannot do the mathematical functions fast or accurately enough for scientists and accountants. This leads to stored function on the calculator and the need for memory.

Some consider an abacus to be the first attempt by mankind to create a computation machine. It consisted of a series of beads on rods that could be manipulated to perform basic mathematical operations such as counting, addition, subtraction, multiplication, and division.

The first major attempt to build an actual computer was by Charles Babbage. Charles Babbage is often referred to as the "father of computing." As a mathematician, he became frustrated with the ever-present errors that came from human-calculated tables and set out to build a machine capable of performing calculations. Although he failed to build a computing machine, he attempted to build two. The first was called the difference engine, which worked with simple calculations. Babbage set out to build this machine to automatically calculate and print accurate mathematical tables. However, he could never get enough funding to complete his machine and eventually abandoned it. Later, he began working on a second machine, the analytical engine, which was to be used to calculate complex equations based on a series of instructions. This machine was also never finished, though it had been started at his death.

The next major step in computing was what are now termed first-generational computers. These were large machines—sometimes taking up full rooms—that could be used exclusively with binary code and could perform only one task at a time. The Atanasoff-Berry Computer (ABC), the ENIAC (Electronic Numerical Integrator and Computer), and the UNIVAC (Universal Automatic Computer) are all examples of first-generation computers.

The Atanasoff-Berry Computer was the first operational computer in the United States. It was limited to one function: solving systems of linear equations. The United States Army developed the ENIAC during WWII. It covered nearly 1800 square feet and could perform basic addition, subtraction, multiplication, and division operations. The UNIVAC was the first computer sold for commercial purposes. It could perform basic mathematical computations and work with letters.

Computer technology's development continued to second-generation computers, which used transistors instead of vacuum tubes (which the first-generation computers did), allowing their size to decrease dramatically.

Third generation computers are characterized by the use of integrated circuits. This dramatically increased the speed and efficiency of computers. In first and second generation computers, the primary, (in some cases the only) method of input and output were punch cards and printouts. Third generation computers were the first computers to feature keyboards, monitors and operating systems.

Fourth and fifth generation computers are still being built today. Fourth generation computers began with the use of the microprocessor. This allowed what took first generation computers a whole rooms worth of space to accomplish to fit in one hand. Companies like Microsoft and Apple started up during this time, and made computers highly commercially successful products. Fifth generation computers involve artificial intelligence, such as voice recognition and neural networks.

A neural network is a type of artificial intelligence which is designed to work like the human brain. They are designed to learn through experience and to store information using interconnected pathways, like the human brain. The interconnected pathways allow any piece of data to be accessed directly, meaning the CPU does have to look through it in order as it does with a regular hard drive.

Pre-Industrial Era
 1900-1926
   In the pre-industrial era, computers became more and more business-oriented, no longer just for scientific use. IBM was founded and computers were used for the first time in war.

1927-1938

Konrad Zuse began research on electric relays to be used as binary code. He built the first computer using digital relays and also the first vacuum tube computer. During this time, magnetic tape was invented and the first logic circuits were built into computers. Claude E. Shannon writes a thesis on computing deemed "Possibly the most important thesis of the twentieth century." Shannon takes 50-year-old math, now called Boolean Algebra and uses it to design a digital computer. Shannon had now given engineers the math they needed to program computers.

During this time, one of the first computer games "Odyssey" was written by Ralph Bear.

Samsung is founded in Korea.

1939

Hewlett Packard is founded.

1944-1946

The first computer is programmed using only punch tape to give commands instead of re-wiring the machine after every new project.
The original "bug" was found in a computer relay. This actual crawly bug caused the computer to not work properly and the term is immortalized.

The term bit is first created.

The Sony Corporation is created.

1947-1961

The transistor is developed and the first stored program computers are created. A/O and FORTRAN are developed. First commercial computers are put on the market. First, Second and Third generation computers are developed. The game Spacewar! is created.

1962-1979

The "C" programming language is developed. Unix is developed. The first CPU is created. ATMs replace tellers in banks. First consumer video game is published. Floppy disk is invented. The first commercial software is released, WordStar and others.

1980-1985

The first portable computer is sold. The game Zork is created. Commodore Vic 20 and 64 sells 20 million+ systems. Apple Macintosh is launched and CD-ROM is created.

1986-1992

Fourth generation computers are created. Computers are evolving according to consumer demands. Video, audio and TV features are created and in demand.

1993

Pentium processor from Intel is launched. Many ISPs are launched.

1994+

Constant monthly, annual improvements, and adaptions in networking, file sharing, the Internet, email, hardware, etc.

Significant People in Computing

Apple Computer Inc. (later shortened to Apple Inc.) was founded in 1976 by **Steven Jobs** and **Stephen Wozniak**. Their first computer, called the Apple I, was a hit among computer enthusiasts but had little practical use. Later, the Apple II and Lisa were released, and both were fairly successful commercially. Then, in 1984 Apple released the Macintosh, the first computer to use a Graphical User Interface (GUI) and mouse. A GUI is an interface which makes it possible for a person to click on an icon and have a program start up. Before GUIs, computers only worked through typed commands. Apple continued improving their products and releasing newer and better ones. Today they are one of the largest computer companies in the world and sell various types of hardware and software.

Bill Gates and his partner **Paul Allen** wrote and created DOS for IBM. They later created Windows followed by many other improvements on the technology including Windows 95, Windows ME, Windows2000 and Windows XP. Bill Gates is a billionaire from his company, Microsoft, which has also created many other software applications, including Microsoft Office which includes Word, Excel, PowerPoint and Outlook, the most popular office applications of all time.

Robert Noyce founded Intel and co-created the first Integrated Circuit (IC). The other co-creator **Jack Kilby** later invented the first pocket calculator for Texas Instruments.

Dennis Ritchie invented Unix, an operating system.

Marc Andreessen co-founded Netscape Communications which brought us Netscape navigator, an Internet browser.

Mitch Kapor founded Lotus Development and later Lotus 1-2-3 (a spreadsheet program).

Bjarne Stroustrup invented programming language C++.

Tim Berners-Lee developed the World Wide Web for CERN (European Council for Nuclear Research) which launched in 1991, so that physicists could swap information easily. He created the standards for HTML, URL and HTTP.

Dan Bricklin and his partner Bob Frankston invented the spreadsheet which revolutionized what useful things could be done on a personal computer. This was the beginning of regular business use of computing.

 Social and Ethical Issues

The latest trends in information systems, especially on-line e-commerce, have increased the profitability of many businesses. The increases in sales and productivity have continued to support the costs of investments in improved technology. Information systems have had a positive economic impact for business. This may or may not be the case for the individual worker whose job may have been replaced by technology. For the worker, the skill level needed to earn a living has increased.

Privacy is a key issue about the proliferation of information systems and databases that store massive amounts of data about each individual. With the ability to link databases and to mine data warehouses, a vast amount of information can be obtained about an individual. According to the American Civil Liberties Union (ACLU), electronic surveillance monitoring of a person's activities while using the Internet is possible and may be a major problem, according to the American Civil Liberties Union (ACLU).

Accuracy of information is another issue. While there is the problem of an individual's data, there is a broader problem concerning the accuracy of disseminated information. People tend to believe what they see on their television or computer. Publishers of print media have been held accountable for the accuracy of what they place in print, but no one verifies the accuracy of what is placed on websites.

Intellectual property, the intangible property in writing, is usually protected by copyright. Copyright problems exist for both software and the written word on the Internet, which provides many items of intellectual property for free that were once sold for a profit.

The history of copyrights goes back to the late 1700s. However, in 1976, new legislation protected intellectual property (including books and software). This legislation mandated that any intellectual property created on or after January 1, 1978, would automatically be protected from the creation date, plus an additional 70 years. Other works, such as anonymous works or works for hire, are protected for 95 years from publication or 120 years from creation, whichever is shorter. It also covers works created but not published with the same protections and time frames.

In 1998, the Digital Millennium Copyright Act was written into law. This new version of copyright protection created two World Intellectual Property Organization (WIPO) treaties, the WIPO Copyright Treaty and the WIPO Performances and Phonograms Treaty, which included additional provisions that addressed other copyright-related issues.

Referred to in a shortened form as DMCA, major areas included in the new protections include:

Making it a crime to circumvent anti-piracy measures built into commercial software, and it outlaws the manufacture, sale, or distribution of code-cracking devices to copy software illegally. However, it is allowed to attempt the cracking of copyright-protection devices in certain cases such as encryption research, product tests, and security tests.
Limits Internet service providers from copyright-infringement liability for simply transmitting information over the Internet, but expects service providers to remove material from users' websites that appear to infringe copyrights.
Limits liability of nonprofit institutions of higher education, when they serve as online service providers, and in certain situations, for copyright infringement by faculty or students.
Updates Section 108 of the Copyright Act of 1976 to accommodate digital technologies and evolving preservation practices. It allows three digital copies of a work to be made, provided that digital copies are not made available to the public outside of the library premises. It also permits a library or archive to copy a work into a new format if the original format becomes obsolete.

Jobs have changed since the introduction of information systems. Job content has changed in many industries as more and more workers perform their jobs through a computerized workstation. Some people consider working with computers all day to be a dehumanizing experience. Commerce is becoming impersonal.

With increased productivity, workers have more responsibilities and with instantaneous transactions the pace of work has increased. Both of these factors contribute to job stress. Repetitive strain injuries such as carpal tunnel syndrome have increased. As information systems proliferate, designers will need to include job design and ergonomics (human factors engineering) as factors in the design of the system.

Business Ethics

Although there may once have been a day when a simple handshake could be considered to ensure a business transaction, business today requires far more monitoring and regulating. The study of business ethics is an attempt to apply moral principles to business operations. Ethics is closely associated with the term morality. Often the two terms are interchangeable, however there is a distinction. Morality is used to describe a person's character. It encompasses their beliefs about behaviors and can dictate how they act or respond in different situations. With morality, the focus tends to be on individuals. Ethics is the study of morality. It focuses on societal acceptance of and adherence to moral principles. Ethics focuses on the social structures which morals are a part of. Ethical principles can be considered generally accepted guidelines or expectations about the way that people (or businesses) behave.

There are three major categories of ethics, all of which come into play in the everyday operations of businesses. Three different schools of ethics are social ethics, economical ethics and legal ethics. Social ethics have to do with the way people interact with one another.

For example, the morality of lying to or stealing from another person falls under social ethics. Economic ethics have to do with business and money related issues. For example, whether or not an American company with overseas offices or factories should have to abide by United States labor laws would fall under economic ethics.

Legal ethics has to do with the actions of lawyers. Things such as lawyer-client privilege fall under legal ethics. For example, one aspect of legal ethics is noisy withdrawals. A noisy withdrawal is when a lawyer becomes aware of fraud committed by their client and withdraws legal representation for their client. They then notify the proper authorities of what they know. For example, in cases involving the SEC, if a lawyer becomes aware of fraud or illegal activities by their client, they should remove themselves and notify the SEC of the wrongdoing.

However, determining ethical principles businesses should follow is not necessarily as straightforward as it sounds. This is because businesses thrive on the ability to generate a profit. Consider, for example, a grocery store. The store purchases the groceries from a supplier. In order to make a profit, the grocery store must sell the groceries for more than it paid for them. At face value, this may seem "wrong" of the company to do; they are knowingly overcharging all of their customers.

However, if they didn't, there would be no grocery stores, and people would have to purchase groceries from the suppliers themselves – a much more difficult process. Therefore, the perceived overcharging, which could be considered unethical, truly benefits everyone involved. Of course, this is a simplified example, and not all business practices can be considered in these terms, nor do they have eventual benefits. Still, it serves to illustrate the point that ethics is not always a cut-and-dry situation. It comes down to that business ethics is a study of the extent to which an action can be viewed as necessary for businesses to thrive and when it becomes entirely unethical.

The Federal Trade Commission Act was passed in 1914. In addition to creating the Federal Trade Commission, it dictated that advertising cannot be deceptive or unfair and must be backed up by evidence. This policy of honest advertising is referred to as truth in advertising.

Many scandals in the early 2000s increased the number of federal regulations involving businesses and lowered people's trust in the business community as a whole. These scandals involved well-known people and companies, including Enron, Tyco International, Martha Stewart, Nike, and WorldCom.

Enron was created in 1985 by the merging of two large gas pipeline companies. By 2000 it had become one of the largest companies in the United States, generating over $100 billion in revenues. Not surprisingly it came as a shock when just a year later (in 2001) the company declared bankruptcy, costing shareholders and investors billions. Under further investigation it was shown that the company had been using accounting practices that were not accurate and showed the company's financial situation in better light than it was by hiding its debt. This was done by creating legal entities called special-purpose entities (SPEs) and then having them assume the debt. This created the impression that Enron had more assets than it did, and that there was a healthy cash flow because the SPEs did not appear on the balance sheet.

Another company associated with accounting scandal is Tyco International. By the end of 2000, Tyco International was a major company, bringing in around 30 billion dollars. The company had three main divisions, involving fire protection, electronics and packaging. When Dennis Kozlowski became the company's Chief Executive Officer (CEO) in the early 1990s he proceeded to expand the business into other industries, and the company soon became one of the largest producers of medical equipment as well.

However, when the SEC launched an investigation of the company, it was discovered that Kozlowski had stolen millions from the company. As one example, he had purchased nearly 20 million dollars of art for himself and used company funds to pay for the art, and the taxes on it. He also threw an extravagant party for his wife using company funds. In total, it was determined that he had stolen around 75 million dollars. In addition, Kozlowski along with the company's Chief Financial Officer, Mark

Schwartz, had arranged to have 7.5 million shares of stock (worth 450 billion dollars) sold without authorization, and then moved the money out of the company and into their own accounts. When the deceit came to light, Tyco International's stock prices dropped by 80%.

The scandals continued as another company, WorldCom, was forced to declare bankruptcy when an internal audit revealed billions of dollars of wrongly reported expenses. The company had been reporting operating expenses as investments. In total, the company had misreported over three billion dollars of expenses as investments. Correcting the financial statements showed that instead of growing, as it had appeared, the company was actually shrinking and in debt. Stock prices fell 99%, once again to the loss of shareholders in addition to over 15,000 people who lost their jobs.

These three incidents shook the securities markets as shareholders lost billions of dollars. The underhanded accounting practices of the three companies resulted in a widespread loss of confidence in the securities market. As a result of this loss of faith, the **Sarbanes-Oxley Act** was passed in 2002. The Sarbanes-Oxley Act tightened laws enforcing accounting and auditing practices with the intent of restoring stakeholder confidence in securities markets.

Another scandal involved Martha Stewart. Stewart built her company from a small gourmet food shop and catering business to founding Martha Stewart Living Omnimedia in 1996. She had become the iconic symbol of a homemaker and the company soon owned multiple magazines, TV programs, books and a newspaper and radio column. However, in 2001 she came under investigation for insider trading. Insider trading occurs when a person trades stock when they have information not available to the general public which influences their actions.

In Martha Stewart's case, the stock in question was ImClone stock, a pharmaceutical company for which her friend, Sam Waksal, was an executive. The day before ImClone's stock value plummeted because it was not given FDA approval for a new drug, Stewart sold off nearly a quarter million dollars of shares, along with Waksal, who sold off nearly five million dollars of shares. Both were eventually convicted of insider trading and Stewart was sentenced to five months in prison and five months under home arrest for her involvement. Insider trading, along with accounting practices, is an aspect considered under business ethics.

The Nike scandal started when it was discovered that the famous athletics brand was producing many of their products in Asian factories with low wages and dangerous working conditions that would not be acceptable in the United States. The company was soon barraged with complaints, and protests were held outside of many of their stores. Within two years their revenue and stock prices had been cut in half. As a result, the company began an exhaustive public relations campaign. They accepted responsibility for the working conditions in foreign factories, and began to work with the factory owners to improve them. They established work codes, and outlined steps to achieving them. In addition, the company went around the country to different universities to restore their image in the eyes of college students.

This scandal raises many questions about business ethics. For example, should United States based companies have to adhere to United States laws even when operating in foreign countries? Also, if so, should this be universally true – or extend only to certain laws? How should child labor, safety codes and wages be addressed? Should the United States based company be held responsible for factory conditions, even if they do not own the factory that supplies their products (as was the case with Nike)? The list goes on, and all of the questions are ones that business ethics seeks to address. However, in many cases there is still not a satisfactory compromise.

Despite the many scandals of the past few decades, the evidence that better ethics actual helps businesses has become increasingly accepted. For example, some of the benefits of doing business ethically are that employees have an increased feeling of loyalty to the company. When employees feel that their company is essentially "good" they are more likely to want to continue working there. A track record of good ethics also increases loyalty from investors. If a company is doing reasonably well, and the investors feel that they can trust the company to be ethical in their practices, they feel more secure in investing in the company.

On the other hand, unethical practices (as shown through the examples above) typically result in downfall of stock prices and loss of profit for the company. By extension, good ethics is therefore healthy for a company's profit. When given the choice between an ethical company and an unethical company, people are more likely to purchase from a company they consider ethical. Consider the example of Nike. Their revenues fell by 50% and people were protesting in front of their stores when they felt like the company was being unethical. Practicing good business ethics has become a way for companies to give themselves a competitive advantage over other companies in their respective industries.

On the large scale, business ethics is also important, but not all ethical problems in business occur between one business and another business or between business and the public as a whole. Some ethical issues apply to the proceedings within business, and these issues also come under the scrutiny of business ethics. For example, issues of conflict of interest, sexual harassment, nondisclosure agreements and discrimination are all addressed by the field of business ethics as well.

Software Licensing

A software license defines any limitations on how consumers can use a program or application. The license may limit the purpose for which consumers can use the program, how many copies consumers can make for their personal use, the process consumers can use to sell their copies of the software, and the modifications consumers can make to the software. Software users may have to agree to the terms of the software license before they can access all of the functions of a computer program or application.

The two main categories of software licenses are open source licenses and proprietary licenses. These types of licenses differ in how they define the ownership of the software copies.

Open source licenses grant the ownership of a copy of software to the end-user. As a result, the consumer of an open source licensed application usually has the right to change, copy, and distribute the software with few or no restrictions. Under proprietary software licenses, the publisher is the legal owner of the software and the consumer owns only a license to use the software.

Under both proprietary and open source licenses, the designer or publisher retains ownership of the software's copyright. Because they do not own the copyright, end-users are usually prohibited from taking credit for the software. In addition, open source licenses may place restrictions on how users must document and distribute changes they make to the software.

Safety and Security for Networks

Businesses and organizations need to implement network security protocols in order to protect their data from accidents and malicious attacks, and to comply with federal, local, or industry-specific regulations.

Networks consist of connected computers, or "nodes." Network security involves controlling who accesses information at each node and as the information travels between the nodes. A network security system has established access rights that define which users or devices are allowed to complete certain functions. Authentication is the process of identifying users and devices, and verifying that they have the required access rights before data is released.

If a computer network is connected to the Internet or to another network, the external connection can be especially vulnerable. A firewall can be installed in the network to inspect data before it travels into or out of the network. The firewall software or hardware functions by denying access to suspicious data.

Mobile Networks

A mobile network is any network whose nodes are connected using wireless technology. For this reason, mobile networks are often called "wireless networks." The nodes of a mobile network may include computers, output devices such as printers, and cellular telephones. These nodes communicate with each other through electromagnetic waves.

The main advantage of a wireless network over a traditional, line-based configuration is portability. Users are able to leave their desk and still access the network. In addition, wireless connections can allow networks to be configured into arrangements that would have been awkward or impossible to implement using traditional connections.

Mobile networks have several drawbacks. Because users do not have to be physically connected to the network to intercept the communication waves, wireless networks are more vulnerable to security breaches. In addition, data flow rate can be significantly reduced over wireless connections. Because there are several different wireless networking standards, linking nodes from different manufacturers or adding new nodes to an existing network can lead to compatibility problems.

Programming Methodology

In computers, a program is a step-by-step set of instructions which tells a computer how to achieve a result. Everything which a computer does requires a program. Creating these programs, or programming, requires knowledge of computer programming languages. Computers understand machine language, or binary code, a system which uses a series of zeros and ones which the computer interprets as instructions. Binary code is tedious and difficult to understand. Because of this, different programming languages have been developed. The use of these languages allows complex programming to take place.

Also for computer programs to work, they must be told how to execute commands they are given. The step-by-step processes which the program follows are called algorithms. For example, if your friend was trying to get to your house, there are likely a number of different ways they could do so. You tell them a specific set of directions for them to follow. This is the algorithm they will follow to get to your house. Computers work the same way, they must be told step-by-step how to do something. If even one step is ambiguous, wrong or missing then the results will not be correct.

Programming methodology is the process of coding software. Before programming can begin, the interfaces, screens, processes, storage files, and outputs for the software should be defined.

Programmers write units of code to produce the interfaces, screens, processes, storage files, and outputs that will compose the software. Each unit is tested individually. As units are completed, they are combined into related functional groups called modules. Each module is also tested to make sure the units are compatible.

As modules are finished, they are connected to produce subsystems. Eventually, all of the modules are integrated to create the complete software. Each time a module is added, the system is tested so that problems with newly added components can be identified.

At each step of the programming process, the software is documented and reviewed. A protocol for testing the completed software is designed.

Designing software is usually performed top-down. This means that the functional requirements for and relationships between every module is defined before the individual algorithms are designed. Programming, however, usually proceeds from the bottom-up, with individual algorithms coded and tested before they are combined into modules, and modules constructed and tested before they are integrated into subsystems. Only after all of the subsystems have been shown to work properly are they joined to create the complete program.

Data Types and Algorithms

An algorithm is a set of instructions for performing a specific task. An algorithm must use a measurable amount of resources and be completed within a definite time. The instructions within an algorithm must be clear and unambiguous. Algorithms can be written using mathematical signs, Boolean logic operators, programming languages, or a pseudo language. Algorithms cannot result in endless loops, continue for an infinite amount of time, or use infinite resources.

A data type is a set of data values along with operations associated with those values. Examples of data types include real numbers, integers, characters, strings, and pointers.

An abstract data type (ADT) is a data type whose definition is not dependent on how it is used by any particular program. A simple ADT is the stack. In a stack, the last data saved is the first data returned. The name "stack" comes from the visualization of the data as a stack of trays, where the tray most recently placed on the stack is on the top and therefore the first to be taken off. Operations associated with a stack include "push," which is used to add a new data element to the stack, and "pop," which returns the most recent element.

The data elements involved in a stack can be integers, strings, pointers, or any other data type including other stacks. Because the definitions for the operations associated with a stack do not depend on what type of data is being stored in the stack, a stack is an ADT.

Another commonly used ADT is the queue. Where a stack accesses data on a "first in, last out" (FILO) basis, a queue is a "first in, first out" (FIFO) structure. The first element added to the queue is the first one that can be accessed. The operators "push" and "pop" are also used on queue structures.

Arrays are data structures whose elements can be accessed by reference to the array name and the position of the element within the array. Arrays can of one or multiple dimensions. In single dimension arrays, an element is accessed using the array name and a single integer that identifies the element's place within the array. The following single dimension array has four integer elements.

ARR = [1, 3, 5, 7]

A programmer could call on any element within the array by referencing the element's position within ARR. In this example, ARR(1) = 1, ARR(2) = 3, ARR(3) = 5, and ARR(4) = 7. Subscripts can also be used to indicate an elements position within an array.

In multidimensional arrays, an element is accessed using the array name and an ordered set of integers. The number of integers required to identify a particular element of an array is called that array's dimension. In arrays of dimension two, the ordered pair used to identify an element lists the row number first and then the column number as shown in the example below.

$$ARR = \begin{vmatrix} 1 & 3 & 5 \\ 7 & 9 & 2 \\ 4 & 6 & 8 \end{vmatrix}$$

ARR(1,1) = 1; ARR(1,2) = 3. ARR(1,3) = 5; ARR(2,1) = 7; ARR(2,2) = 9; ARR(2,3) = 2; ARR(3,1) = 4; ARR(3,2) = 6; ARR(3,3) = 8.

Program Concepts

Although computer languages differ in how they implement operations and data structures, there are several concepts common to every language.

Regardless of the language used, programs rely on variables for temporary storage of numbers, characters, and other data types. A variable is used to hold data that is inputted or calculated at one point in an algorithm and will be outputted or further processed later in the algorithm.

There are two types of variables: global and local. Global variables are in scope, or able to be read and modified, throughout the entire program. Local variables are only in scope for a defined part of the program, such as a function or subroutine. Although the variable itself cannot be accessed or changed by parts of the program for which the local variable is not in scope, the value of the variable can be passed to other functions or subroutines.

In programming, a string is a finite sequence of terms. Multiple strings can be stored as arrays. An array is a single variable which has many different terms or variables stored in it, similar to a box which is divided into multiple sections. Arrays are helpful when there are multiple related elements. The computer can look in one place for the information instead of multiple places. A loop is a command which repeats itself, either indefinitely or until a series of requirements are met.

Programmers use loops to tell the computer to follow a list of instructions multiple times. A loop can be a condition, counted, or infinite. In a condition loop, the computer checks a variable or set of variables against a defined condition. If the variables pass the condition test, the instructions within the loop are performed. After each completion of the loop, the condition is checked again. When the variables fail the condition test, the instructions within the loop are not carried out and the loop ends. Consider the following simple loop:

```
WHILE X > 0
LOOP
X=X-1
END LOOP
```

If X=5 at the start of the loop, the loop would be completed five times. After the fifth iteration, X would equal 0. The condition test would not be passed and the instructions within the loop would not be carried out.

The terms WHILE or UNTIL in a program indicate a condition loop.

A counted loop is one that is performed a set number of times. In many higher level programming languages, the terms FOR and NEXT are used to create a counted loop. The FOR statement is used to create a counter. NEXT instructs the computer to advance the counter by one. The following counted loop would be repeated five times.

```
FOR X=1 to 5
        A=A+1
        B=B+1
NEXT
```

By defining a counting variable before the loop, a counted loop can be written as a condition loop. The following conditional loop is equivalent to the counted loop sample above:

```
X=1
WHILE X<6
LOOP
            A=A+1
            B=B+1
X=X+1
END LOOP
```

Sometimes, either by design or through error, a loop may be repeated until the computer turns off or an error closes the program. Loops that do not end by themselves are called endless or infinite loops. The following pseudocode is an example of an endless loop. The condition that signals the start of the loop is always true.

```
X=1
WHILE X>0
LOOP
            A=A+1
            B=B+1
X=X+1
END LOOP
```

Logic Concepts

Computer algorithms use logic conditions to define how to treat data. Logic conditions are used to test data then carry out instructions based on the results of the test. Some common tests performed on data include:

- Equals (= or ==): The data being tested is equal to the value of a given static or variable.
- Not equals (!=): The data being tested does not equal the value of a given static or variable.
- Less than (<): The data being tested has a lower value than that of a given static or variable.
- Greater than (>): The data being tested has a higher value than that of a given static or variable.

In most circumstances, the data being tested must be compared to a static or variable of the same data type. Some programming languages will automatically convert the type of the data being tested if it does not match the comparison data. For example, if the program compares a character to an integer, the character may be converted into an integer based on its ASCII value.

More complicated tests can be performed using logical, also called Boolean, operators to relate data. The Boolean operators are and (&&), or (||), and not (!).

Logic tests are performed using the IF statement and variations of the IF statement. The syntax used to code an IF statement is dependent on the computer language used. However it is coded, an IF statement follows a basic process:

IF (the result of a logic test is true) THEN (do action X)

The following table shows some simple logic tests using test data A and a given variable B.

IF Statement Logic Tests

Symbolic Representation	Explanation
IF A=B, THEN Y	If A equals B, then do action Y
IF A!=B, THEN Y	If A does not equal B, then do action Y
IF A>B, THEN Y	If A is greater than B, then do action Y

IF A>||=B, THEN Y   If A is greater than or equal to B, then do action Y
IF A<B, THEN Y   If A is less than B, then do action Y
IF A<||=B, THEN Y   If A is less than or equal to B, then do action Y
IF A=0 || B=0, THEN Y   If A equals 0 or B equals zero, then do action Y
IF A=0 && B=0, THEN Y   If A equals zero and B equals zero, then do action Y

There are three common variations to the IF statement: ELSE, ELSE IF, and CASE. The ELSE statement defines an alternative action to take if the test fails.

IF (the result of a logic test is true) THEN (do action X) ELSE (do action Y)

ELSE IF provides the rules for an additional test if the previous test fails.

IF (the result of a logic test is true) THEN (do action X)
ELSE IF (the results of a different logic test are true) THEN (do action Z)

CASE statements are used to provide action rules for tests with several outcomes.

>   CASE 1: Do action X
>   CASE 2: Do action Y
>   CASE 3: Do action Z

A CASE statement is the equivalent to a series of ELSE IF statements. The example CASE statement above can be rewritten using ELSE IF commands.

>   IF (the result of logic test 1 is true) THEN (do action X)
>   ELSE IF (the result of logic test 2 is true) THEN (do action Y)
>   ELSE IF (the result of logic test 3 is true) THEN (do action Z)

CASE statements are sometimes called SELECT or SWITCH statements.

Software Development Tools

Software development tools are applications that automate tedious programming tasks or facilitate complicated functions. Four commonly used software development tools are compilers, debuggers, documentation generators, and integrated development environments.

Compilers translate code written in one programming language into another programming language. Programs written in a high-level language such as C++ or Turbo Pascal must be translated into assembly or machine language in order to be executed by the computer. Although code may be compiled by hand, the process is slow, complicated, and prone to errors.

A debugger is a software development tool that allows programmers to step through lines of code, track the values of variables, and locate instructions that lead to crashes. Debuggers make it easier for programmers to find and correct errors in programs.

Documentation generators use information about the design and implementation of applications to produce user guides and programming documentation. Documentation generators speed up the task of gathering screens, forms, source code files, and data flow diagrams.

An integrated development environment (IDE) is an interface for software development tools. Using an IDE can help programmers work more efficiently by reducing the need to switch back and forth between development tools.

 # Sample Test Questions

Test questions are an additional way to learn the material for your test. All the questions and answers that follow may not necessarily be covered previously in the study guide. However, this is information that you will need to know for the test. If you are unfamiliar with the answer, skip the question and come back to it. By using the answer key at the end of this sample test, you will have the correct answers and will be able to study the correct information for the exam.

1) What can Internet users use to find web pages for which they don't know the address?

   A) Uniform Resource Locator
   B) ISP
   C) Search engine
   D) Database

The correct answer is C:) Search engine. A URL would be used if they already knew the address.

2) An 8 bit video card can display how many colors?

   A) 8
   B) 16
   C) 64
   D) 256

The correct answer is D:) 256.

3) Which programming language creates applets?

   A) C++
   B) JavaScript
   C) PERL
   D) Java

The correct answer is D:) Java. Applet is the name given to the programs which are created using Java.

4) Which job function oversees the timeliness, budget and schedule of a project?

   A) Project manager
   B) Software engineer
   C) Network administrator
   D) Data analyst

The correct answer is A:) Project manager.

5) What is a string?

   A) A ten character set of numbers.
   B) A variable which has multiple variables within it.
   C) A finite sequence of terms.
   D) A command to repeat a process.

The correct answer is C:) A finite sequence of terms. A ten character set of numbers could be a string, but it is not an encompassing definition.

6) URL stands for

   A) Ultimate Resource Location
   B) Ultimate Relation Location
   C) Uniform Resource Locator
   D) Uniform Relation Locator

The correct answer is C:) Uniform Resource Locator.

7) Which of the following is NOT true of ENIAC?

   A) It was the first fully programmable electronic computer.
   B) It was completed in 1946.
   C) It was also known as the Colossus.
   D) All of the above are true.

The correct answer is D:) All of the above are true.

8) Screen resolution is described in units of

   A) Inches
   B) Centimeters
   C) Pixels
   D) VPNs

The correct answer is C:) Pixels.

9) What type of software allows tracking of costs, timelines and events related to projects?

   A) Presentation
   B) Project management
   C) CAD
   D) RAD

The correct answer is B:) Project management.

10) Who founded Apple Computer Inc.?

   A) Steven Jobs
   B) Bill Gates
   C) Stephen Wozniak
   D) Both A and C

The correct answer is D:) Both A and C. Bill Gates is a cofounder of Microsoft. Steven Jobs and Stephen Wozniak founded Apple.

11) What type of software converts handwriting to text on the computer?

   A) OCR
   B) MICR
   C) Biometric Device
   D) ORC

The correct answer is A:) OCR.

12) Which of the following is NOT an output device?

   A) Mouse
   B) Speakers
   C) Screen
   D) Printer

The correct answer is A:) Mouse. A computer mouse is an input device.

13) Which of the following is NOT an image file type?

   A) GIF
   B) BMP
   C) JPEG
   D) JOT

The correct answer is D:) JOT.

14) What distinguished second generation computers from first generation computers?

   A) The use of microprocessors instead of transistors.
   B) The use of vacuum tubes instead of microprocessors.
   C) The use of transistors instead of integrated circuits.
   D) The use of transistors instead of vacuum tubes.

The correct answer is D:) The use of transistors instead of vacuum tubes. This allowed the size of the computer to decrease significantly.

15) Which of the following is an output device?

   A) Printer
   B) Mouse
   C) Keyboard
   D) Scanner

The correct answer is A:) Printer.

16) The Digital Millennium Copyright Act of 1998 is divided into five titles. Which of the following is NOT a title of DMCA?

   A) WIPO Copyright and Performances and Phonograms Treaties Implementation Act of 1998
   B) Online Copyright Infringement Liability Limitation Act
   C) Computer Maintenance Competition Assurance Act
   D) All of the above are titles of DMCA

The correct answer is D:) All of the above are titles of DMCA.

17) POS terminals are found everywhere BUT the following?

   A) Grocery store
   B) Gift shop
   C) Clothing store
   D) Office building

The correct answer is D:) Office building.

18) Which of the following is an example of volatile memory?

   A) Hard drives
   B) RAM
   C) ROM
   D) All of the above

The correct answer is B:) RAM. Hard drives and ROM (Read Only Memory) are both non-volatile.

19) What word below is part of a mathematical formula to encrypt information?

   A) Hash
   B) Encode
   C) Macro
   D) Password

The correct answer is A:) Hash.

20) Where does the CPU search first?

   A) L1 cache
   B) L2 cache
   C) Hard drive
   D) RAM

The correct answer is A:) L1 cache. Generally the L1 cache is directly attached to the CPU.

21) Which job function creates and codes computer applications?

   A) Project manager
   B) Software engineer
   C) Network administrator
   D) Data analyst

The correct answer is B:) Software engineer.

22) DRM stands for

   A) Database Rights Management
   B) Data Rights Management
   C) Domain Rights Management
   D) Digital Rights Management

The correct answer is D:) Digital Rights Management.

23) Which job function works with the engineers to create documentation for the product?

   A) Graphic designer
   B) Desktop publisher
   C) Technical writer
   D) Analyst

The correct answer is C:) Technical writer.

24) Which of the following correctly lists the symbols which may NOT be used for naming Windows documents?

    A) <, >, :, ", /, \, ?, & and *
    B) <, >, :, %, /, \, ^, ? and *
    C) #, $, %, ", /, \, ^, ? and *
    D) <, >, :, ", /, \, |, ? and *

The correct answer is D:) <, >, :, ", /, \, |, ? and *. These nine symbols may not be used. However, ?, &, $, # and % may.

25) Which of the following would NOT be used in association with a MIDI device?

    A) Keyboard
    B) Speakers
    C) Scanner
    D) Software

The correct answer is C:) Scanner.

26) A compiler will translate information from one language, called the source language, into another language, called the

    A) Target language
    B) Final language
    C) Expected language
    D) End language

The correct answer is A:) Target language. This is the language that the program should end up in.

27) Electronic components that make up the computer such as the monitor are called?

    A) Hardware
    B) Software
    C) CPU
    D) Desktop

The correct answer is A:) Hardware.

28) Which of the following titles would NOT indicate an image file?

   A) JPEG
   B) GIF
   C) PNG
   D) BIF

The correct answer is D:) BIF. These are boot information files.

29) Which of the following is an input device?

   A) Keyboard
   B) Monitor
   C) Printer
   D) Power supply

The correct answer is A:) Keyboard.

30) Which of the following is another name for a website address?

   A) WAN
   B) ISP
   C) IP address
   D) URL

The correct answer is D:) URL. WAN is a wireless area network, ISP is an Internet service provider and IP address is the computer's address, not the website's.

31) A relational database stores data in the form of

   A) Lists
   B) Tables
   C) Webs
   D) Files

The correct answer is B:) Tables.

32) Why are arrays useful?

   A) The computer could not function without arrays because they give the instructions about how to execute commands.
   B) They tell computers to continue performing a command until the requirements are met, meaning the computer user doesn't have to watch the program continually.
   C) They are a mathematical shortcut which allows the computers to cut down on execution time.
   D) They allow the computer to find all the information about a specific thing in one place, so it doesn't have to search for each piece individually.

The correct answer is D:) They allow the computer to find all the information about a specific thing in one place, so it doesn't have to search for each piece individually.

33) A master control program that oversees all the functions of the computer is called?

   A) OS
   B) ALU
   C) RAM
   D) ROM

The correct answer is A:) OS.

34) A person wishing to view web pages will most likely use which protocol?

   A) File Transfer Protocol
   B) HyperText Transfer Protocol
   C) URL protocol
   D) None of the above

The correct answer is B:) HyperText Transfer Protocol.

35) Which device can information NOT be read from and rewritten?

   A) ROM
   B) RAM
   C) Floppy disk
   D) Thumb drive

The correct answer is A:) ROM.

36) What was the first functional computer in the United States?

   A) UNIVAC
   B) ENIAC
   C) Atanasoff-Berry Computer
   D) Abacus

The correct answer is C:) Atanasoff-Berry Computer. It was followed by the ENIAC and then UNIVAC a short time after.

37) Someone who tries to illegally access your computer files would be called a

   A) Sniffer
   B) Mummy
   C) Hacker
   D) Caster

The correct answer is C:) Hacker.

38) A person sends an e-mail and makes it appear as though it were coming from someone else. This is called

   A) Hacking
   B) Pharming
   C) Spoofing
   D) Phishing

The correct answer is C:) Spoofing. Spoofing is when a person alters or obscures their identity.

39) What is the component that supports the standard arithmetic function like add and subtract as well as logical operations like AND and OR?

   A) CPU
   B) DOS
   C) ALU
   D) RISC

The correct answer is C:) ALU.

40) Which of the following is NOT a rule of proper netiquette?

   A) Title e-mails with descriptive subjects.
   B) Never type in all capitals.
   C) Always read messages before forwarding.
   D) Never use emoticons.

The correct answer is D:) Never use emoticons. Emoticons are allowed, as long as they aren't overused.

41) The reverse of downloading information is called

   A) Streaming
   B) Flowing
   C) Outsourcing
   D) Uploading

The correct answer is D:) Uploading.

42) A neural network is designed to work like

   A) A car engine
   B) The human brain
   C) The nervous system
   D) A political entity

The correct answer is B:) The human brain. They are designed to learn and store information using interconnected pathways, like the human brain.

43) A beta version of software is created for

   A) Purchase by end users
   B) Scientists
   C) Programmers
   D) Testing by end users

The correct answer is D:) Testing by end users.

44) Which of the following cases involves voluntary computer control?

   I. When a person hacks another computer.
   II. When a person creates a zombie computer.
   III. When a person creates a slave computer.

   A) I and II only
   B) II and III only
   C) III only
   D) I, II and III only

The correct answer is C:) III only. Hacking and zombie computers both involve involuntary computer control.

45) How many bits are in a byte?

   A) 1
   B) 2
   C) 4
   D) 8

The correct answer is D:) 8.

46) A programmer writes a program in C++. In order to understand it, the computer uses a program to translate it into binary code. The program that does this is called a(n)

   A) Translator
   B) Compiler
   C) Interpreter
   D) Interchange device

The correct answer is B:) Compiler. Compilers translate information into machine language.

47) Binary-coded decimals are stored as ___-bit binary number?

   A) 1
   B) 2
   C) 3
   D) 4

The correct answer is D:) 4.

48) Which is NOT considered a characteristic of a good algorithm?

   A) Precision
   B) Uniqueness
   C) Finiteness
   D) Specificity

The correct answer is D:) Specificity.

49) Which of the following is NOT an example of network architecture?

   A) Star
   B) Ring
   C) Bus
   D) Train

The correct answer is D:) Train.

50) Which of the following is NOT a programming language?

   A) PERL
   B) HTML
   C) CGI
   D) Java

The correct answer is C:) CGI. CGI is an important and distinct element, but can be written in many different languages.

51) When data is transmitted at very high speeds by using circuits that synchronize data transfer with electronic clock signals it is called

   A) Asynchronous
   B) Synchronous
   C) Full-duplex
   D) Echoplex

The correct answer is B:) Synchronous.

52) ARPANET was

   A) The first successful Internet.
   B) A WAN set up by the Department of Defense.
   C) A LAN set up by the Department of Justice.
   D) None of the above

The correct answer is B:) A WAN set up by the Department of Defense. It played a useful role in the development of Internet.

53) Also called local echo, this asynchronous transmission can only handle one signal at a time, alternating between two computers

   A) Full-duplex
   B) Half-duplex
   C) Echoplex
   D) Parallel

The correct answer is B:) Half-duplex.

54) Which of the following is NOT a classification of hardware?

   A) Input device
   B) Motherboard
   C) Output device
   D) Storage device

The correct answer is B:) Motherboard. The motherboard is a piece of hardware, but it is not a classification of hardware.

55) Sound based signals that can be transmitted over the telephone lines

   A) Digital
   B) Modem
   C) Dial tone
   D) Analog

The correct answer is D:) Analog.

56) A person sends fake e-mails which appear to be from another person's bank, asking them to confirm their credit card information and passwords. This is called

   A) Hacking
   B) Pharming
   C) Spoofing
   D) Phishing

The correct answer is D:) Phishing. Phishing is when a hacker sends an e-mail which leads people to a site which looks legitimate and asks them to enter personal information.

57) This occurs when the system is powered on

   A) Cold boot
   B) Warm boot
   C) Reboot
   D) Medium boot

The correct answer is A:) Cold boot.

58) What are the step-by-step processes which computers follow called?

   A) Programs
   B) Algorithms
   C) Netiquette
   D) Software

The correct answer is B:) Algorithms. Algorithms are the instructions which tell computers how to execute instructions.

59) What is it called when both an old and new system are used simultaneously for conversion to a new system?

   A) Parallel conversion
   B) Phased conversion
   C) Pilot conversion
   D) Plunge

The correct answer is A:) Parallel conversion.

60) Refresh rate is

   A) The number of times per minute that the screen is updated.
   B) The number of times per second that the screen is updated.
   C) The number of times per year that the screen is updated.
   D) The number of times per millisecond that the screen is updated.

The correct answer is B:) The number of times per second that the screen is updated. Refresh rate is measured in Hz.

61) A handheld computer that is customized for everyday functions for personal organization is called a

   A) PGA
   B) PDA
   C) PC
   D) CPU

The correct answer is B:) PDA.

62) Which of the following statements is TRUE?

   A) Pipelining is when the CPU works on multiple tasks simultaneously.
   B) Pipelining is useful and speeds up computer function.
   C) Pipelining is an out of date practice which slows down computer functions.
   D) Both A and B

The correct answer is D:) Both A and B.

63) Ergonomics in computing is

   A) The science of programming
   B) The science of making something easy to use
   C) The science of seating
   D) The science of network language

The correct answer is B:) The science of making something easy to use.

64) A fax machine sends information

   A) Over the Internet
   B) Through a telephone wire
   C) Via satellite
   D) Any of the above

The correct answer is B:) Through a telephone wire.

65) What uses symbols to represent programs or computer functions?

   A) COBOL
   B) BASIC
   C) GUI
   D) JPEG

The correct answer is C:) GUI.

66) Which of the following correctly orders the steps which the CPU follows in executing a command?

   A) Fetch, Execute, Decode, Writeback
   B) Fetch, Decode, Execute, Writeback
   C) Fetch, Writeback, Execute, Decode
   D) Decode, Writeback, Execute, Fetch

The correct answer is B:) Fetch, Decode, Execute, Writeback.

67) Which is NOT a procedural programming language?

   A) FORTRAN
   B) BASIC
   C) COBOL
   D) Java

The correct answer is D:) Java.

68) HTML is a(n)

   A) Internet protocol system
   B) Programming language
   C) Uniform Resource Locator
   D) None of the above

The correct answer is B:) Programming language. HTML stands for Hyper Text Markup Language.

69) This software package supports production of documents

   A) Data management software
   B) Word processing
   C) Desktop publishing
   D) Graphics software

The correct answer is B:) Word processing.

70) What is the distinguishing feature of fifth generation computers?

   A) Artificial intelligence
   B) Microprocessors
   C) Integrated circuits
   D) Hand held devices

The correct answer is A:) Artificial intelligence. This includes features such as neural networks and voice recognition software.

71) This software incorporates photographs, diagrams and other images with text to produce sophisticated documents

   A) Data management software
   B) Word processing
   C) Desktop publishing
   D) Graphics software

The correct answer is C:) Desktop publishing.

72) Which of the following statements is TRUE?

   A) Non-volatile memory is erased when the computer is turned off.
   B) Volatile memory is erased when a new program is initiated.
   C) Non-volatile memory is erased when a new program is initiated.
   D) Volatile memory is erased when the computer is turned off.

The correct answer is D:) Volatile memory is erased when the computer is turned off. For example, RAM is volatile memory.

73) This software provides real-time transcription of voice

   A) Data management software
   B) Word processing
   C) Desktop publishing
   D) Speech recognition software

The correct answer is D:) Speech recognition software.

74) Information travels over the Internet in small units of information called

   A) Beta particles
   B) Internet units
   C) Packets
   D) Integrated circuits

The correct answer is C:) Packets.

75) This software allows the user to convert data to a graphical form

   A) Data management software
   B) Word processing
   C) Desktop publishing
   D) Graphics software

The correct answer is D:) Graphics software.

76) Which type of image file is most used in pictures because of its ability to display smooth color transitions?

   A) JPEG
   B) MPEG
   C) GIF
   D) PNG

The correct answer is A:) JPEG. GIF and PNG are high contrast image files and MPEG files are video files.

77) Which of the following is NOT a database data model

   A) Hierarchical
   B) Network
   C) Relational
   D) Query language

The correct answer is D:) Query language.

78) ARPANET developed

   A) HTTP protocols for transmitting data.
   B) Packet switching for efficiency when transferring data.
   C) Implementing antivirus software and firewalls.
   D) All of the above

The correct answer is B:) Packet switching for efficiency when transferring data.

79) _____ is a program that embeds itself into another program and infects a personal computer when the other program runs.

   A) Virus
   B) Trojan
   C) Red pill
   D) Trojan horse

The correct answer is A:) Virus.

80) Which of the following is NOT an input device?

   A) Keyboard
   B) Fax machine
   C) Scanner
   D) Microphone

The correct answer is B:) Fax machine. A fax machine is an output device.

81) Microsoft Excel is an example of what type of program?

   A) Word processing software
   B) Desktop publishing software
   C) Spreadsheet software
   D) Graphics software

The correct answer is C:) Spreadsheet software.

82) Why are multiple small caches used?

   I. Because one large cache would be too bulky.
   II. Because the CPU can search faster when the caches are small.
   III. Because the technology for one large cache hasn't been developed.

   A) I only
   B) I and II only
   C) I and III only
   D) II only

The correct answer is D:) II only.

83) Microsoft Word is an example of what type of program?

   A) Word processing software
   B) Desktop publishing software
   C) Spreadsheet software
   D) Graphics software

The correct answer is A:) Word processing software.

84) What is the maximum length of a Windows file's path name?

   A) 100 characters
   B) 260 characters
   C) 500 characters
   D) 1000 characters

The correct answer is B:) 260 characters.

85) Adobe InDesign is an example of what type of program?

   A) Word processing software
   B) Desktop publishing software
   C) Spreadsheet software
   D) Graphics software

The correct answer is B:) Desktop publishing software.

86) Which of the following resolutions will offer the most clarity?

   A) 50 x 150
   B) 730 x 1000
   C) 840 x 1240
   D) 930 x 1360

The correct answer is D:) 930 x 1360. The more pixels there are, the higher the resolution, and the higher the resolution is, the clearer it will be.

87) Adobe Photoshop is an example of what type of program?

   A) Word processing software
   B) Desktop publishing software
   C) Spreadsheet software
   D) Graphics software

The correct answer is D:) Graphics software.

88) Which of the following is NOT a classification of software?

   A) Application software
   B) System software
   C) Interpretation software
   D) Programming software

The correct answer is C:) Interpretation software. Application, system and programming software are the three classifications of software.

89) _____ provides access to a remote computer for retrieval of files.

   A) FTP
   B) EDI
   C) URL
   D) TCP

The correct answer is A:) FTP.

90) Distributed denial of service attacks are performed through

   A) Servers
   B) High powered computers
   C) Slave computers
   D) Zombie computers

The correct answer is D:) Zombie computers. A distributed denial of service attack is when a hacker creates many zombie computers which are used to overload a site and make it crash.

91) When you do the action CTRL+C what happens?

   A) An item is copied
   B) An item is cut
   C) An item is deleted
   D) An item is saved

The correct answer is A:) An item is copied.

92) Which of the following charges a periodic fee?

   A) URL
   B) IP
   C) ISP
   D) TCP

The correct answer is C:) ISP. The other three answers all relate to the Internet, but only the ISP charges a fee.

93) When you copy something to the clipboard, it will remain there until

   A) It is pasted
   B) It is sorted
   C) It is replaced
   D) It is collated

The correct answer is C:) It is replaced.

94) A person finds free software on the Internet, but when they go to download it they discover that it has deleted all of their files. This software would most correctly be called a

   A) Virus
   B) Worm
   C) Trojan horse
   D) None of the above

The correct answer is C:) Trojan horse. It appeared useful, but actually harmed the computer.

95) Which type of software is free for the public to download and use?

   A) Public-domain software
   B) Shareware
   C) Freeware
   D) Peer-to-peer

The correct answer is A:) Public-domain software.

96) What stage is the CPU in when it produces output?

   A) Writeback
   B) Fetch
   C) Execute
   D) Decode

The correct answer is A:) Writeback. This could include displaying an image on a screen, playing music through speakers, printing, or many other operations.

97) Someone who appears legitimate but is in fact soliciting financial information from you or your passwords is called a

   A) Sniffer
   B) Phisher
   C) Tracker
   D) Caster

The correct answer is B:) Phisher.

98) A person makes it so that when people try to access a specific website, they are redirected to a fake one. This is called

   A) Hacking
   B) Pharming
   C) Spoofing
   D) Phishing

The correct answer is B:) Pharming.

99) Which job function installs and monitors LANs?

   A) Project manager
   B) Software engineer
   C) Network administrator
   D) Data analyst

The correct answer is C:) Network administrator.

100) What was unique about the Macintosh when Apple first released it?

   A) It was the first computer with Internet access.
   B) It was the first commercially successful computer.
   C) It was the first computer to incorporate a GUI and mouse.
   D) It was the first program based computer.

The correct answer is C:) It was the first computer to incorporate a GUI and mouse.

101) The Copyright Act of 1976 protected works for how long?

   A) From the moment of creation
   B) Term of the author's life
   C) The term of the author's life plus 70 years
   D) All of the above

The correct answer is D:) All of the above. This legislation protects a work from the moment of creation (without requiring publication) for the term of the author's life plus an additional 70 years.

102) Hertz is equal to cycles per

   A) Second
   B) Minute
   C) Hour
   D) Schedule

The correct answer is A:) Second. Hertz is equal to cycles per second.

103) In computer science, the value between 1 (true) and 0 (false) is known as

   A) Middle
   B) Average
   C) Fuzzy
   D) None of the above

The correct answer is C:) Fuzzy. Fuzzy logic is used in programming to determine something that has to be quantified between 0 and 1.

104) The Digital Millennium Copyright Act allowed libraries to make how many digital copies of a work?

A) One
B) Two
C) Three
D) Four

The correct answer is C:) Three. DMCA allows for libraries to make up to three copies of a work provided that digital copies are not made available to the public outside of the library.

105) Which of the following is used to interrogate the database and retrieve groups of records for analysis?

A) HTML
B) PHP
C) SQL
D) SKYPE

The correct answer is C:) SQL. SQL stands for structured query language.

106) The intent of the Sarbanes-Oxley Act was to

A) Help companies be better able to deal with the ethical problems raised by increased technology.
B) Restore stakeholder confidence in the securities market after a series of scandals in the early 2000s.
C) Create a commission that would monitor the accounting records of major businesses.
D) Scare businesses into conforming with the GAAP standards in their accounting practices.

The correct answer is B:) Restore stakeholder confidence in the securities market after a series of scandals in the early 2000s.

107) A gigabyte equals how many bytes?

   A) One thousand
   B) Ten thousand
   C) One million
   D) One billion

The correct answer is D:) One billion.

108) Which of the following statements is FALSE?

   I. A virus generally requires human action to spread.
   II. A virus can be harmless or malicious.
   III. A virus attaches itself to e-mails only.

   A) I and III only
   B) II only
   C) II and III only
   D) III only

The correct answer is D:) III only. A virus attaches itself to files, not just e-mails.

109) An example of a biometric device is

   A) Fingerprint scanner
   B) Optical mouse
   C) Infrared
   D) Body language sensor

The correct answer is A:) Fingerprint scanner.

110) A refresh rate lower than what will cause a noticeable flicker?

   A) 20 Hz
   B) 50 Hz
   C) 60 Hz
   D) 100 Hz

The correct answer is C:) 60 Hz.

111) A person wishes to copy an image from a piece of paper onto a computer. They would need to use a(n)

   A) Scanner
   B) Output device
   C) Fax machine
   D) Printer

The correct answer is A:) Scanner. A scanner is an input device. It is used to get an image from paper to the computer screen.

112) Apple Computer was founded in 1976 by _____ and _____.

   A) Alan Turing, Aaron Greenspan
   B) Steve Jobs, Steve Wozniak
   C) Steve Martin, Steve Carell
   D) Bill Gates, Paul Allen

The correct answer is B:) Steve Jobs, Steve Wozniak. Apple was founded in 1976 and incorporated in 1977 by Steve Jobs and Steve Wozniak to sell Wozniak's Apple I computer.

113) In order to convert seconds to milliseconds, an _____ must be used.

   A) Apple
   B) Addend
   C) Algorithm
   D) Admin

The correct answer is C:) Algorithm. An algorithm is a quick, simple way to make calculations.

114) A _____ is a system that has been compromised and can be used remotely to perform malicious tasks, frequently without the owner's knowledge.

   A) Trojan horse
   B) DDOS
   C) Server
   D) Zombie computer

The correct answer is D:) Zombie computer. Much like zombies, a virus can cause a computer to be corrupted and controlled to perform malicious attacks.

115) Preventing unauthorized access while allowing outward communication is a function of a _____.

   A) Router
   B) VPN
   C) Proxy server
   D) Firewall

The correct answer is D:) Firewall. A firewall is a security measure that protects a network by blocking unauthorized use but allowing authorized systems to communicate outwardly.

116) _____ is the sending of fraudulent emails as a way to collect personal information, whereas _____ directs users to fraudulent websites to collect personal information.

   A) Phishing; pharming
   B) Phase encoding; phablet
   C) Phreaking; phonon
   D) Phubbing; phun

The correct answer is A:) Phishing; pharming. Phishing is fraudulent emails, pharming is direction to fraudulent websites. Both attempt to look as authentic as possible to collect personal information.

 Test Taking Strategies

Here are some test-taking strategies that are specific to this test and to other DSST tests in general:

- Keep your eyes on the time. Pay attention to how much time you have left.
- Read the entire question and read all the answers. Many questions are not as hard to answer as they may seem. Sometimes, a difficult sounding question really only is asking you how to read an accompanying chart. Chart and graph questions are on most DANTES/DSST tests and should be an easy free point.
- If you don't know the answer immediately, the new computer-based testing lets you mark questions and come back to them later if you have time.
- Read the wording carefully. Some words can give you hints to the right answer. There are no exceptions to an answer when there are words in the question such as always, all or none. If one of the answer choices includes most or some of the right answers, but not all, then that is not the answer. Here is an example:

    The primary colors include all of the following:
    A) Red, Yellow, Blue, Green
    B) Red, Green, Yellow
    C) Red, Orange, Yellow
    D) Red, Yellow, Blue

Although item A includes all the right answers, it also includes an incorrect answer, making it incorrect. If you didn't read it carefully, were in a hurry, or didn't know the material well, you might fall for this.

- Make a guess on a question that you do not know the answer to. There is no penalty for an incorrect answer. Eliminate the answer choices that you know are incorrect. For example, this will let your guess be a 1 in 3 chance instead.

 Test Preparation

How much you need to study depends upon your knowledge of the subject area. This book is much different than the regular DANTES study guides. This book actually teaches you the information that you need to know to pass the test. The book follows the outline of the knowledge and skills required for the subject matter as stated in the regular study guide. It is important to understand all the major concepts that are listed in the table of contents and it is very important to know any words in bold print.

One of the fallacies of other test books is test questions. People assume that the content of the questions are similar to what will be on the test. **That is not the case.** They are only to test your "test taking skills" so for those who know how to read a question carefully, there is not much added value from taking a "fake" test.

To prepare for the test, make a series of goals. Allot a certain amount of time to review the information you have already studied and to learn additional material. Take notes as you study; it will help you to learn the material.

Legal Note

All rights reserved. This Study Guide, Book and Flashcards are protected under the US Copyright Law. No part of this book or study guide or flashcards may be reproduced, distributed or stored in a retrieval system, or transmitted in any form or by any means, electronic, mechanical, photocopying, recording, or otherwise, without the prior written permission of the publisher Breely Crush Publishing, LLC.

FLASHCARDS

This section contains flashcards for you to use to further your understanding of the material and test yourself on important concepts, names or dates. Read the term or question then flip the page over to check the answer on the back. Keep in mind that this information may not be covered in the text of the study guide. Take your time to study the flashcards, you will need to know and understand these concepts to pass the test.

Hardware	Software
CISC	ALU
Hard drive	RAM
ROM	Input device

Any program that runs on the computer	Anything that makes up the computer like the monitor, etc.
Arithmetic Logic Unit	Complex Instruction Set Computer
Write and read memory	Stores information
Keyboard, mouse	Read Only Memory

Peripheral device	POS
Output device	PDA
Bit	Byte
EBCDIC	ASCII

Point of Sale	Scanner, printer
Personal Digital Assistant, ex. a Palm Pilot	Anything that retrieves information from the hard disk like the printer or monitor
Eight consecutive binary digits	Each binary digit
American Standard Code for Information Interchange	Extended Binary Coded Decimal Interchange Code

JPEG	TIFF
MPEG	LAN
Ring network	WAN
Asynchronous	Cold boot

Tagged Image File Format, another type of image file	Image file
Local Area Network	Movie Picture Experts Group, digital video files
Wide Area Network	A network where each node is "daisy chained" to the next node so all connect in a ring
When the system is powered on and restarted by a user	Sending one bit after the other

RAD	**PERT**
Gantt Chart	**Pseudocode**
What are the logical operators?	**Name 2 object-oriented languages**
Name 4 procedural languages	**HTML**

Program Evaluation and Review Technique	Rapid Action Development
Simple and standardized programming language	A chart used in project management which shows the amount of time for each step in the development process
C++, Java	And, or, not
HyperText Markup Language	FORTRAN, BASIC, COBOL, C language

Example of an input device	Peripheral device
Blog	Plunge
SQL	Kilobyte
MHz	Encryption

Any electronic component that is attached to the computer but external to it	Keyboard
Abrupt changeover to a new system without using one of the other conversion techniques first	Online journal or webpage where a person (or company) posts anything they want
1000 bytes	Structured Query Language
Modifying data so that it cannot be deciphered with the encryption key	1 million cycles a second

Firewall	**Storage device**
Application software	**Programming software**
System software	**Graphical User Interface (GUI)**
Slave computer	**Zombie computer**

A classification for hardware which stores information in a computer, such as the hard drive or RAM	A barrier between your computer and other computers. It scans incoming data to be sure it meets security requirements and protects against hackers
A classification for software which is designed to help programmers write programs more effectively and efficiently	A classification for software which is designed to help a computer user accomplish a task
A computer interface which facilitates human and computer interaction through the use of a screen and mouse	A classification for software which runs the computer
A computer which a hacker has taken control of and uses to perform illegal or destructive actions	A computer which a computer owner has networked with another which then controls it

Screen resolution	**Uptime**
Token ring	**Hub**
Virtual Private Network (VPN)	**Mail merge**
Interpreter	**Compiler**

A measure of the availability of a server	A description of the clarity of a screen based on pixels
A piece of hardware through which computers in a LAN are connected	A network in which computers are linked in a circle and information must be passed one at a time around the circle
A program used to create large amounts of documents which are identical, but have a few unique elements	A private network in which computers are connected through a public network
A program which translates a program written in a computer programming language into machine language	A program which executes instructions in a computer programming language

Java	Netiquette
File Transfer Protocol (FTP)	Antivirus software
Neural network	Blu ray
Radio waves	MPEG

A set of guidelines dictating what is or isn't proper to do online	A programming language which is used to create selfcontained programs, called applets, which can be put onto a web page
A software which scans the programs already on the computer for anything dangerous	A set of protocols for transferring files over the internet
A type of disc with higher storage capacity than CDs or DVDs used for high definition videos	A type of artificial intelligence which is designed to work like the human brain
A type of file used for digital videos	A type of electromagnetic wave which is used for satellite transmission

PNG	**GIF**
Search engine	**Online Transaction Processing (OLTP)**
Decision Support System (DSS)	**ARPANET**
Machine language	**Expert system**

A type of image file used for images with sharp contrasts between colors and which supports simple animations	A type of image file used for images with sharp contrast between colors which does not support animations, but has a larger color range than GIF
A type of program which allows real time online transactions to occur	type of internet search aid used by computer users which finds web pages matching the user's request
A WAN set up by the Department of Defense which played an integral part in the development of internet protocols	A type of software used to help managers or business people to interpret data and make decisions
An application that has been developed using AI methods that have been applied to a highly specific area of knowledge and is capable of giving advice about that area	Also called machine code or binary code. A language created entirely using zeros and ones which is the language computers understand

MP3	Volatile memory
CPU	CSO
CAD	EIS
HTTP	Public domain

Any type of memory which is erased when the computer is turned off	An audio file
Chief Security Officer	Central Processing Unit. A piece on the motherboard which is essentially responsible for running the whole computer
Executive Information System. This displays information from other databases in easy to read charts and graphs.	Computer Aided Drafting or Design. This is used in software or engineering applications.
Information which is not copyrighted and is available for free and open public use	HyperText Transfer Protocol. The protocol for how servers and computers communicate. Used for the display of web pages

ISP	Charles Babbage
OIS	Pharming
Cascading Style Sheets (CSS)	Random Access Memory (RAM)
Packets	Cell

Known as the "father of computing" he was the first person to attempt to build a computation machine	Internet Service Provider. Any company which offers internet access in exchange for a periodic fee.
Pharming is when a hacker makes it so that when you try to go to a website it is secretly redirected to another fake website.	Office Information System
Short term, volatile memory used by computers to avoid the slower hard drive	Programs which allow web designers to more easily manipulate and control the appearance of a web page
The area where a row and column in a spreadsheet intersect	Small units of information which are used in transferring data over the internet

Pipelining	Pixel
Downtime	TCP/IP
URL	Outsourcing
Phishing	Spoofing

The smallest identifiable element which composes the images on a computer screen	The process through which a CPU is able to work on multiple tasks simultaneously
Transmission Control Protocol/Internet Protocol	This is when the server or system is unavailable due to acrash or maintenance
When a company moves part of their business to another location, generally in another country.	Uniform Resource Locator. The website address
When a person alters or obscures their identity online	When a hacker sends an email which leads people to a site which looks legitimate and asks them to enter personal information

www.ingramcontent.com/pod-product-compliance
Lightning Source LLC
Chambersburg PA
CBHW081831300426
44116CB00014B/2555